DINING WITH
THE DOCTOR

Dining With The Doctor

The Unauthorized Whovian Cookbook

Chris-Rachael Oseland

ISBN: 978-1481153683

First Edition

Table of Contents

THINGS YOU SHOULD KNOW

HELLO, SWEETIE

Thanks for taking a chance on my labor of love. I've spent the last year watching and rewatching the entire reboot of Doctor Who. Amazingly, I still love it. Since you bought this book, I know you do, too.

There are a few things you need to know before you turn another page.

SPOILERS!

This book includes a recipe for every episode of the reboot. I did my best to keep each recipe genuinely relevant to the episode, so yes, there are spoilers in every single recipe. I'm not too worried about this since it's safe to assume anyone who owns this cookbook loves the show as much as I do. However, if you're a new fan, stop reading before you reach your latest episode. You've been warned.

EPISODE NUMBERING

You'd be surprised how many different ways the episodes are numbered. The Christmas specials are sometimes thrown in with the previous series and sometimes treated as the first episode of a new series. Other places list them in a sort of seasonless limbo. The Series 4 David Tennant specials are just an incredible mess. In the end, I went with what I considered the clearest, most easily understood system I could find. Your mileage may vary.

AMERICAN VERSUS METRIC MEASUREMENTS

You can tell by the spelling and volumetric measurements that I am, in fact, an American. I've done my best to convert all my recipes into their metric equivalents. It's only fair. You gave us Doctor Who. I practically owe you recipes you can make without keeping a calculator in the kitchen.

However, despite my best intentions, going back and forth between a measurement based on volume and one based on weight can be tricky. When in doubt, always fall back on the sad, non-standard, antiquated American measurements.

SPECIAL DIETS

Most of the Doctor Who themed recipes on the web are for startlingly gorgeous desserts. Unfortunately, that makes them off limits to people with Celiac disease (who can't eat wheat), people who are lactose intolerant (who can't have dairy), vegetarians (who can't eat meat) vegans (who can't eat any animal byproducts, including eggs or dairy) and paleo or low carb dieters (who can't eat grains.) I've gone out of my way to make sure there are a few recipes everyone can eat. Check the appendix for help finding recipes which fit your needs. If you're on a special diet, by all means, feel free to modify any of my recipes to fit your need, then please post the changes online for everyone to share.

SERIES 1: LAST OF THE TIME LORDS

Nestene Consciousness (S1, E1 - Rose)

4 cups/950 ml cream
3 cups/710 ml red wine
2 cups/475 g sugar
2 lemons or limes
1 sprig rosemary

Hello, Doctor. It's been awhile. You're looking very modern in your black t-shirt and leather jacket - and if you don't mind me saying so, kind of sexy with those high cheekbones and that sparkle in your eye. You're trouble. I like it.

You're back on Earth, more than a little scarred from the Time War, and very much needing some bright, optimistic human company again. You found that, but you also found a Nestene Consciousness. While bright and colorful, it wasn't so friendly.

My fellow fans, you too can stare into a suspicious vat of thick orange and red. Drinking this won't leave you possessed by an alien, though if you down the whole batch, you might start hearing voices.

Confidentially, this recipe is a modified syllabub - a fine historic mixed drink that also doubled as a dessert, because our ancestors knew how to party.

The texture of a fully frothed red wine syllabub bears a striking resemblance the Nestene Consciousness. Drink enough of them and you'll also think you hear a menacing voice coming from your glass.

Start by mixing your wine, citrus and sugar until you have an undrinkable mess. Don't worry. Once they're well blended, you're going to dilute the dense concoction by pouring in heavy cream.

The Doctor no doubt would've witnessed an 18th century household servant spending hours with a whisk properly beating the cream into an edible froth. Today, the miracle of modern technology allows you to pour everything into a bowl and attack it with a hand mixer set to medium high. After a mere ten minutes your Nestene Consciousness should start to transform into a striking red whipped cream.

Once you've worked it up into a good, angry froth, layer the mix into tall glasses with a wide bulb on top, such as Guinness pint glasses or ice cream float glasses.

Let your alien lava drink sit in the fridge for about four hours while fluid separates out from the cream. You should end up with a dark, red-black liquid layer lurking beneath a cloudy red layer of sweet, fleshy foam. Serve it with a long, bendy straw and bad intentions.

The Last Human Fruit Leather (S1, E2 - The End of the World)

1 1/2 pounds/700 grams ripe pears
1/4 cup/60 ml water
2 tbsp/13 g sugar
2 tsp/30 ml fresh lemon juice
1/4 tsp/1 g ground cinnamon
pinch salt
gummy/candy brains
candy googly eyes and lips

The first time I rewatched this episode I wanted to make a glorious sculpted beef head with a broccoli crown that spiraled up to red bell pepper flowers. Then I remembered that would be a tremendous pain the ass without being the slightest bit recognizable to anyone who wasn't totally obsessed with beautiful women who die within 30 screen minutes of meeting The Doctor. Instead, I decided Cassandra should remain the star of this episode. Fruit leather is a lot easier to make, and once you throw some googly eyes on her, Cassandra is a lot more instantly recognizable.

Start off by heating your oven to 170F/80C. If your oven doesn't go that low, just make do with your lowest setting and occasionally let some heat escape by propping the door open a smidge. (You can also use a food dehydrator if you happen to have a slightly smelly two headed aunt who gives you random electronics.) While your oven is barely warming, peel, core, and dice your pears. Toss them in a saucepan. They look so lonely in there. Throw in the water, sugar, cinnamon and salt to keep them company. Bring the whole mess to a boil, all while stirring with a rubber spatula. Once it's boiling, turn the heat down to a simmer and let the water break down the cellular walls of the pears for the next 20 minutes. Give the mix an occasional stir.

You should now have a nice pear paste. Scoop it all into a blender, add the lemon juice, and give it a good spin. It should take less than a minute for your pear lumps to turn into pear puree. Now spread a piece of waxed paper on a baking sheet. It may seem redundant, but go ahead and add a little nonstick spray. Trust me. Once your paper is well lubricated, pour a neat rectangle of pear blend about 1 inch/2.5 cm from the edge of the sheet then fill in the middle with the rest of the blender's contents. Use your rubber spatula to spread it all into a nice, thin, even layer.

Slide the baking sheet into the oven and wait for six to seven hours. Yes, really. Dehydration takes time. You can make this a couple days in advance, which is a good thing because there's nothing more boring than waiting for fruit leather to dehydrate. Paint dries faster. Well, watercolors do. Acrylics are dicey. Oil paints will take days. What I'm really trying to say is that if you sit around waiting for your fruit leather to dehydrate you'll have hours on your hand to come up with even worse analogies. Go enjoy life instead. When you come back from your exciting adventures in time, space, and comparative paint dehydration, you should have a nice sheet of not-quite-white-enough homemade fruit leather. You may look at the fruit leather and think it looks disturbingly like Cassandra spent some time in a tanning bed. Confidentially, if you want that milky white complexion, you can avoid the hassle of making fruit leather and just rip a slice of store bought mozzarella cheese in half. I won't tell. We both know you're going to read a lot of these recipes, skim for store bought cheater sections, and agree that you'll make the complicated recipe when you have more time. Some day. Honest. Right now, though, it's all about appearances. Don't worry. I won't judge. Just be warned that thin slices of cheese are notoriously difficult to keep on display without them ripping into a messy, confusing pile.

Whether you're using the fruit leather or grocery store cheese slices, rip it into artistic rectangles with rough edges. Now take an extra thick bamboo skewer and carefully spear the bottom and top, as though you're making a sail to hang on the mast of a pirate ship. Tug your fruit leather as straight as possible on the skewer. Now put some store bought edible eyes and lips around where Cassandra's face should go. If you're extra artistic, you can get edible paint pens (yes, those are real things) and draw on a face and eyes. Now plunge the wide end of the skewer into a largeish candy brain. These are readily available in the United States around Halloween. If you can't find any candy brains, just use the miniature square candy bar of your choice. What you're looking for here is some stability to hold Cassandra up. If your stability is in the form of a brain, it looks more like the episode, but no one will dock you points for missing that detail.

I got about 16 Cassandra clones from my batch of fruit leather. A dozen of them didn't even rip when I skewered them. If you really love fruit leather, you can make up to 4 pans of it at a time. Your imperfect fruit leather scraps can be reused as a garnish for the Liquid Flesh Cocktail from Series 6, The Almost People. Just make some crude paper dolls out of brown paper bags and stuff the fruit leather faces in the top. Now you have instant Gangers as well as Cassandra.

Charles Dickens Own Christmas Punch (S1, E3 - The Unquiet Dead)

1/2 gallon/1.9 liters bottled mineral water
1 750 ml bottle dark rum
1 350 ml bottle brandy
2 cups/220 g brown sugar
3 large lemons
cinnamon sticks
grated nutmeg

This authentic recipe from the author of the world's best known Christmas story is strong enough to animate a walking corpse (at least in Cardiff). No matter where you live, this is a tasty, dramatic, nicely alcoholic drink that will impress the guests at your next Doctor Who Christmas Special party.

To make it, gently warm your rum and brandy in a saucepan. The goal is to warm it up, not boil off the alcohol. When the brandy is unpleasantly warm to the touch, add in the sugar and stir until it dissolves. Once the sugar granules are nothing but a ghost of sweetness past, add in the zest and juice of your lemons.

Let this simmer gently on the stove for ten minutes.

Just before serving, remove it from the heat and add the bottled mineral water. If you're feeling fancy, you can cut out a wheel of lemon to put at the bottom of each glass. Fill the glass with punch, spike the lemon with a cinnamon stick, and top it with a sprinkle of nutmeg. Dickens described the cinnamon, nutmeg, and lemon wheels as optional, so feel free to experiment until you find your favorite combination. It might take you several drinks.

Since Dickens did have a flare for the dramatic, he also offered an alternate serving method.

Instead of pouring his punch into individual glasses, bring the painfully hot pan to the table and pour the contents into a large, fire-proof bowl. The last part is important if you don't want to be drinking liquid plastic.

Float a ladle full of brandy on top of the punch. Refill the ladle with even more brandy and carefully ignite the surface. Ever so slowly, pour the flaming brandy into the punchbowl. If all goes well, your waterfall of flame will set the punch in the bowl on fire. If not, you'll look a bit pretentious, but under the circumstances, no one will be terribly surprised.

Extinguish the flames by giving the bowl a good, hearty stir, then ladle your warm, no longer flaming drink into glasses prepared with your choice of lemon wheels or cinnamon sticks. Once everyone has a glass in hand, settle in for a night of holiday ghost stories.

Slitheen Killing Beans on Toast (S1, E4 - Aliens of London)

1/2 can Heinz baked beans in tomato sauce
2 slices white bread
2 eggs
as much butter as you can stand (or 2 tbsp/30 grams)

British readers, you're entirely forgiven for wondering why Americans, known for their love of starchy foods, find beans on toast to be strange, alien, and exotic. For you, beans on toast is a comfort food. For most Americans, it might as well be served with a Slitheen egg.

I'm going to justify this recipe to folks in the UK by pointing out a few facts about Slitheen anatomy. The acetic acid in both the beans and the catsup is toxic to Slitheen.

That would be enough justification for chowing down, but let's be honest, the gas exchange in their suits produced nonstop comical farts.

You can either chow down with impunity and pretend the after effect of a bean filled meal is part of your clever Slitheen costume or you can suspiciously eye your fellow diners, insisting anyone who won't try your plate of beans on toast must be an alien bent on human destruction. To make it a really Whovian (and slightly cannibalistic) plate, substitute the hard boiled Slitheen Eggs recipe for the fried eggs here.

From this point on, this barely deserves to be called a recipe. Pour your can of beans into a pot to warm them up. Americans, you absolutely must go to the UK section of your grocery's international aisle and pick up some Heinz Baked Beans. Our assorted baked beans, while glorious with barbecue, don't taste anything like theirs. Spend one whole extra dollar for the imported taste.

Throw an obscene amount of butter into a skillet and fry up your eggs. Once the eggs are done, throw some more butter in and fry up your toast. If your arteries aren't hardening in anticipation, you're doing it wrong. Once your toast is golden brown, spread it on a plate, pour about half the can of beans on top, slide your fried eggs over the beans, and serve with extra catsup, Worcestershire sauce, and plenty of hot tea. If you're still alive in the morning, you're probably human.

Slitheen Skin Suits (S1, E5 - World War Three)

6 firm, green Bartlett pears
6 large green (seed-in) grapes
1 cucumber
handful of very small blueberries

Admit it. The Slitheen look like walking pears. Sometimes it seems like the alien designers at Doctor Who came up with a lot of their concepts over lunch. I can imagine the designer of the baked potato inspired Sontarans staring forlornly into his bagged lunch, hoping for inspiration, when he pulled out a pear. Yes, he thought. That's it. Who cares that the name Slitheen sounds like it belongs on some great snake headed beast with a terrible lisp? What Doctor Who needs is a race of giant farting pears. I'll get right on that after lunch. God, I love my job.

Luckily for us, it's pretty easy to make your own miniature (fart free) alien out of a pear. In fact, it's so easy I hesitate to call this a recipe. I'm not sure how else to label a set of foods with specific preparation instructions, though, so humor me.

This recipe turns into a quick easy, edible table decoration that should be instantly recognizable to anyone who enjoys the Eccleston years.

Pick out six particularly potbellied pears with long, strong stems. Grab one of your larger seed-in grapes (they're about twice the size of seedless ones) and push it onto the stalk to represent the alien's improbably tiny head. It's looking like a Slitheen already! Now use your fingernail (or a small paring knife if you're feeling extra precise) to dig out some eye holes then fill them up with some small, dark blueberries. I found the frozen ones work best. You can really shove them into the grape without worrying about the frozen berries losing shape. Interestingly, my frozen berries are also about half the size of fresh blueberries, which makes them surprisingly useful for adding eyes to food. Fair warning: I tried just drawing eyes and a mouth on using icing. It just slid right off the grape's smooth skin.

Make arms by peeling your cucumber skin into long, wide strips then draping them from the shoulders of your pear down around the bottom of the belly. Get out a paring knife and trim the cucumber strips into oversized green arms. If you're feeling extra precise, carve one end into big, clawed hands. I held my arms in place with toothpicks. To hide the toothpicks, snip off the exposed part then use the tine of a fork to push the wood into the flesh of the cucumber. Make sure to warn your guests before they bite in.

These are a nice, cheap, relatively easy recipe. Once you get the hang of it, you can whip up some Slitheens surprisingly fast. When pears are in season, they're an instantly recognizable dish nearly guaranteed to make your fellow Whovians giggle.

Banana Dalek (S1, E6 - Dalek)

Nutella
banana
Pocky Sticks
mini marshmallows
cotton swabs
cinnamon candy
rock candy

I love everything about this recipe. First, if you've never tried bananas dipped straight in Nutella, I apologize for the five pounds you're about to gain. Second, our friends the Daleks are back! Since The Doctor says you should always bring a banana to a party, this recipe is a great way to celebrate the return of everyone's favorite somewhat modernized upended trash cans on wheels.

Find the straightest, firmest yellow bananas. These are usually the extra large, long ones. The good thing about going big is you can usually get two Daleks out of every banana.

You're going to need a steady hand and some self control.. It is way too easy to make a Dalek, eat a banana dipped in Nutella, make another Dalek, then prepare to exterminate the deliciousness of one more Nutella dipped banana before it attacks the human race

Before the sugar shakes set in, cut your first banana in half. If it's super curvy, go ahead and carve the top into a more Dalek shaped head. I used the tines of an extra wide fork to cut three horizontal lines into the head. With a steady hand, cut some equally shallow vertical lines down the length of the Dalek's body.

If you're a little quivery from eating half the pot of Nutella you might need some help for the detail work. I use a cotton swab dipped in Nutella to make a line of characteristic dots down the body of my Daleks. Somehow, mine always end up a little sloppy. I like to blame the sugar. If you want a neater look, you can substitute mini chocolate chips pushed into the banana. If you do that, I advise filling the vertical skirt lines with Nutella. It both enhances the look and gives you an excuse to use more Nutella. Trust me. Where Nutella is concerned, any excuse is a good one.

You have a few options for finishing it off. I like to make the plunger arm out of a Pocky stick and the eggbeater arm out of either a coffee stirrer or a cotton swab.

If you're a dedicated Whovian, you'll make the eyestalk out of a small pretzel stick with a Cheerio on the end. Dip the Cheerio in the Nutella to both get the right color and make it stick. If you're lazy, just shove a cinnamon candy in the middle of the Dalek's face and call it a day.

When I can find extra tiny marshmallows (the type you typically see in hot chocolate packets) I dip one end into the Nutella (in order to glue them onto the banana) and use them as stubby little antennae. To be honest, this is an imperfect science at best. You can also snip the ends off another cotton swab and plug those into the head for the antennae. Make sure to warn people not to eat the cotton swabs. Sure, cotton is technically edible, but the sticks are entirely the wrong kind of crunchy. Mind you, I'd eat rocks dipped in Nutella, so your guests may not care.

Spread a layer of Nutella on a platter. This will mostly help glue your banana Daleks in place (they're prone to a bit of wobble.). I advise picking up some rock candy. You can strategically arrange it around the platter to help add an otherworldly atmosphere and, far more importantly, help hold your less stable bananas upright.

Once you get the hang of etching lines into the bananas, these whip up faster than you think. Sadly, they won't exterminate your hunger. In fact, much like the Dalek's themselves, once you see these bananas, you'll only want more.

Satellite 5 Mystery Takeout Noodles (S1, E7 - The Long Game)

1 lb/450 g linguine, spaghetti, or angel hair pasta
1 cup/200 g peanut butter
6 scallions (green onions), thinly sliced
2 tbsp/30 ml peanut or vegetable oil
2 tbsp/30 ml soy sauce
2 tbsp/30 ml sesame oil
1 ½ tsp/8 ml white vinegar
1/4 tsp/2 g ground red pepper
1/2 of a red bell pepper, cut into thin strips
½ cup/100 g green cabbage, sliced thin
3 garlic cloves, minced
1 tsp/5 grams salt

Welcome to Satellite 5! We're all about the news here. If you have time to eat, you have time to work. What, you want a Cronk Burger? Too much time wasted chewing! Try some Zaffik instead. Rose says it tastes like a beef slushie.

Oh, you like to occasionally chew your food? Well, grab a box of noodles, then. They're served cold so you can't tell if they're fresh or two days old.

Just eat it and run !

The great thing about this Blade Runner-esque recipe is you can reuse it for a lot of other Doctor Who themed recipes.

Sure, if Eccleston is your favorite Doctor you can always get some Chinese takeout boxes, sharpie on the number 5, then serve these cold noodles with a side of French Onion soup in a sippy cup. Or, you can still serve some of the noodles out of a homemade Satellite 5 takeout box while using the rest as a base for other recipes, like the River Song.

Luckily for a busy person like you, this recipe is that it's so simple even Rose's friend Bruno Langley could make it.

Boil the pasta according to package directions. While it's merrily boiling away, put your peanut butter and vegetable oil in a large, microwave safe bowl and nuke it until the peanut butter is runny. That takes about 30 seconds, a good stir, and 30 more seconds in my microwave, but your wattage may vary. After 1 minute, stir and check it every 20 seconds. The goal here isn't boiling hot peanut butter. You just want something runny enough to cheerfully absorb the other flavors.

Once your peanut butter is cooperatively soft, mix in the soy sauce, sesame oil, vinegar, red pepper, salt, and minced garlic cloves. Once everything is pretty smooth, add in your thinly sliced red bell pepper and cabbage.

By now, your pasta is probably done. If not, glare bitterly at the water until it properly infuses the noodles with delicious softness. Once they're ready, strain the noodles and run cold water over them to stop them cooking. If you're saving some for another recipe, set them aside now. Dump the rest into your peanut butter mix. Give everything a good, hearty stir so the noodles will be thoroughly covered.

Now, you can technically eat them while warm, but that defeats the purpose of a cold noodle recipe. Go put them in the fridge for at least an hour (or up to two days). That gives the flavors some time to mingle and soak into the pasta. They're now ready to be piled into Satellite 5 takeout boxes or stealthily used in other recipes. Never, ever miss an opportunity to point out you're using leftovers from Satellite 5 with some meat picked up in Manhattan Park's Hooverville and washing it down with a cocktail you picked up at Donna Noble's first wedding. Anyone who doesn't get the references doesn't deserve to be at your party.

Pete Tyler's Health Tonic (S1, E8 - Father's Day)

8 cups/2 l brewed green tea
4 tbsp/60 ml honey
1 tsp/5 g salt
Juice of 1 tangerine
Zest of 1 tangerine
1 cucumber, cut into ¼ inch/.63 cm slices

Well, Rose, there's good news and bad news.

The bad news is your father was actually a scam artist. The good news is, in an alternate dimension where he never knocked your mother up, he became an incredibly successful entrepreneur. Don't take it personally.

In our universe, Pete Tyler sold "Vitex," a real world health tonic that was pretty much snake oil. In Ricky's universe next door, though, he was so wildly successful we have to assume he actually came up with some original recipes of his own.

Therefore, you can proudly serve your guests this electrolyte enhancing, Vitamin C rich, surprisingly tasty health tonic. It may not extend their lives long enough for the Cybermen to start offering "upgrades," but it'll certainly give be refreshing on a long, hot summer day.

Brew 8 cups/2 liters of strong green tea. While that's brewing, cut a whole cucumber into ¼ inch slices and dump them into a large pitcher. Zest your tangerine (orange part only. Avoid the nasty white interior pith) and toss that into the pitcher. When you're done zesting, squeeze the juice out of your tangerine like you're milking the last remnants of individuality from a Cyberman's soul and add that to the pitcher, too. Add your honey and salt. These are your "electrolyte balancing" items. Seriously, "electrolyte" infused drinks just have ample sugar and salt added. That's it. Everything else is green food coloring and artificial flavors.

In this case, Pete's all natural electrolyte beverage offers you some genuine tastiness as well as the sugars and salts your body craves. It also happens to be tasty. Now stop worrying about pseudo-scientific terms and pour your brewed green tea over the lot.

Give it a good, solid stir. Let the mix sit at room temperature for a minimum of 4 hours, or up to 1 day. (If you left that nasty white pith on your fruit, you'll regret it. It'll turn the whole mix undrinkably bitter.) The longer you let this sit, the cloudier it becomes, so if you want a nice, crystal clear beverage, make it the same day you plan to serve it. After 4 or more hours, strain out all the solids. Pete's tonic is now ready to be served to your adoring masses.

This freezes really well. If you have any leftover, make it into ice cubes and use them to flavor your water. Be warned, if you're trying to increase your daily water intake, these make downright addictive ice cubes. Maybe that's how Pete Tyler got so rich.

Wartime Cheese and Potato Dumplings with Fried Spam Slices (S1E9 - 10 The Empty Child/The Doctor Dances)

One of the best Science Fiction convention costumes I ever spied was a steampunk couple who simply gave their little boy a gas mask. It was almost impossible not to back away a couple of steps when he walked up and asked, "Are you my mummy?"

By the time this episode aired, I was already sold on the show's reboot, but the two-parter made me really believe the new Doctor Who had legs. It was beautifully written, so wonderfully atmospheric, and used the now classic technique of making something ordinary into something terrifying. Little did I know this would be my first step down the path towards feeling instantly suspicious of things like shadows and statues.

I feel almost guilty critiquing their London Blitz Scavenger's Meal. Almost. Even on the black market, a table like the one we saw full of roast pork, carrots, potatoes, and brown gravy in such generous portions would've been nearly impossible. In reality, a hearty Blitz era feast would've consisted of cheese and potato dumplings with pan fried spam slices and wartime ration bread toasted in the extra grease from the spam drippings.

To give you a real idea what Londoners actually survived on during the Second World War, take a look at the weekly ration allowance for one adult in the 1940's.

Bacon & Ham 4 oz
Meat to the value of 1 shilling and sixpence (around about 1/2 lb minced beef)
Butter 2 oz
Cheese 2 oz
Margarine 4 oz
Cooking fat 4 oz
Milk 3 pints
Sugar 8 oz
Preserves 1 lb every 2 months
Tea 2 oz
Eggs 1 fresh egg per week
Sweets/Candy 12 oz every 4 weeks

That's it. If you ate it all, you went hungry until next week. It's amazingly austere. I could easily use all those ingredients to make a single meal with modest servings for four. Other than strictly rationed items, the grocery stores stocked limited quantities of flour, beans and potatoes. People were encouraged to dig up their gardens and plant vegetables and herbs, which certainly helped. Even raisins were a scarce treat.

Out of sheer respect for people who lived through the Blitz (and love for these two episodes) I humbly present the sort of authentic Air Raid meal Nancy and her pack of lost kids might've actually found while the householders were hiding in their bomb shelters. I'll admit I decadently doubled the amount of herbs (and added salt, pepper, and more herbs to my baked potato peels), which is probably why the end result tasted far better than I expected.

Wartime Cheese and Potato Dumplings with Fried Spam Slices

2 lbs/900 g of potatoes
2 eggs
4 oz/114 g grated cheese
½ tsp/2-3 g salt
¼ tsp/1-2 g pepper
1 tbsp/15 g of any dried herbs you've grown, such as thyme, basil, or parsley

Wash and peel the potatoes. If you want to really get a feel for the blitz, save the potato peels. You'll rub them in any leftover cooking grease you can find, dust them with any leftover crumbs and and spices from the plates, then bake them up as a crispy treat. Nothing was wasted.

First, though, cube your potatoes and boil them in lightly salted water. Once they're fork soft, put them in a colander and let them drain naturally for 10 minutes. You want to let the starches rest before you mess with them again. Set the potato water aside as a soup base for your next meal.

After the potatoes have rested and you've set aside the water they boiled in, return the potatoes to your saucepan. Keep the heat low while you add your salt, pepper, and herbs. Give it a good stir. Add both the eggs (or, if you're feeling extra authentic, two reconstituted powdered eggs) and half the cheese then give it another good stir. Keep stirring until the potatoes firm up. If you happen to have some extra flour, you can always add a tablespoon/15 grams of it to help thicken the dumplings.

Heat your oven to 350F/178C. Turn the potato mix into 12 small balls, roll them in the remaining grated cheese, then put them on a lightly greased baking tray and let them cook for 20 minutes until they're brown and crusty.

While they're baking, open your tin of Spam and cut it into ½ inch/1.25 cm slices. Spam has a nice, high fat content, so you don't need to waste any of your precious cooking fat. Fry the slices on a medium-high heat until they're crispy on each side.

When the spam slices are done, you have to make a decision. If you have any leftover Wartime Loaf (a very simple bread) you can use the leftover spam grease to fry up a slice for each family member. Add it to their plate along with the dumplings and spam slices.

If you're out of bread, get the potato peelings and rub them into the spam grease until they're as well coated as possible. Add whatever salt and herbs you can spare. Spread the peelings into a thin layer on a baking sheet and put them in the oven for 10 minutes. This should work out well. The dumplings take 20 minutes to cook. If you fry the Spam for 10 minutes, then bake the potato peels for 10 minutes everything will be ready for the table at the same time.

Everyone should get 2 slices of Spam, 3 potato dumplings, and either 1 slice of fried toast or 1 handful of baked potato peelings. Chow down on this wartime meal while staring out your window and wishing a wheezing blue box would appear outside your door.

Slitheen Eggs (S1E11 - Boom Town)

4 cups/1 liter water
6 large white eggs
6 bags (or 6 tsp/30 g loose) black tea
1 tbsp/15 g green peppercorns
2 whole cloves
1 star anise
1 cinnamon stick
2 tbsp/30 g white sugar
1 inch/2.5 cm peeled fresh ginger, sliced thickly
16-20 drops green food coloring

Okay, so these are a little smaller and a little less tentacly than Margaret was when she regressed to childhood, but they're also not sentient, which means you don't need to feel guilty about chowing down on these marbled green eggs.

Start by bringing the water to a boil.

Add the green tea, star anise (or 1 tsp/5 grams regular anise), cinnamon stick and peeled ginger. Once the water is nice and bubbly, let the tea brew for about 5 minutes then soft boil your eggs.

To soft boil the eggs, reduce the boiling tea mix to a simmer then gently lower in your eggs one at a time. (You can use this same recipe to make a dozen eggs. No need to double anything but the eggs themselves.) Cook them for 8 minutes with the lid on. Now, carefully remove your eggs from the pan and rinse them in cold water so you don't burn your hands. Once they're cool to the touch, use the back of a spoon to gently crack the shells. You don't want to peel the shells off or break them into pieces. Just tap away with the spoon to create a nice crackle pattern in the surface. The more you crack them, the more intricate and interesting the pattern.

Now add the green food coloring, sugar, and peppercorns (if you can't find green pepper, go ahead and substitute whatever mixed color peppercorns are locally available) to the pan and gently lower the cracked eggs into the water. Bring the mix back up to a boil then turn the heat down to low. Put a lid on and leave the eggs in the brew for the next 40 minutes.

When you pull them out, you'll have green eggs with an amazing brown veined pattern. If you use white eggs, the interior of the peels are even more impressive than the exterior. Best of all, the eggs themselves with have a really neat but subtle flavor. These will remain good in the fridge for a couple of days, so feel free to make them in advance. They taste best warm or at room temperature, though.

Since your Slitheen eggs don't have any of Margaret's tentacles, when you're ready to serve them, boil a mix of half black and half whole wheat angel hair pasta according to the package directions. If your local grocery doesn't have black pasta, don't stress over it. Just get the whole wheat type. The two colors combine to look more like the overall effect of the texture and color of the tentacles, but no one is going to be that big a stickler for details. You can also pick up black squid ink pasta on Amazon.

Toss your pasta in a little olive oil, fresh garlic, and salt (the oil helps keep your pasta from drying out as well as acting as a vehicle for the flavor) then make it into some neat little nests. You're welcome to substitute your favorite olive oil based sauce if you want a flavor with more punch. A tomato based sauce will make it look like you stabbed the living egg until it bled on your pasta. If you really hated Margaret (and your friends have strong stomachs) then go right ahead. A white sauce just doesn't work. Trust me.

Snuggle an unpeeled Slitheen egg into each nest. Let people peel the eggs at their plate so they get the full effect of the green, veined outside as well as seeing the artistically colored inside. As cool as the unpeeled eggs look, the inside of the shells really sell the overall alienness. Once you're done showing off, you end up with a unique, mellow, spicy flavor that tastes just as alien as it looks.

This makes a good main course for your vegetarians and lactose intolerant friends. As an added bonus, even if you special order the squid ink pasta, you still have a dirt cheap main dish with a nice, dramatic flair. Be warned, people who eat eggs tend to ask for extras (as much to play with as to eat) so go ahead and make some spares.

Big Brother House Bad Wolf Brand Human Chow Cookies (S1E12 - Bad Wolf)

1 cup/225 g unsalted butter, room temperature
1 cup/210 g light brown sugar
1/3 cup/65 g white sugar
2 large eggs
1 tsp/5 ml vanilla extract
1 1/2 cups/195 g flour
1 tsp/5 g baking soda
1 tsp/5 g salt
½ tsp/3-4 g cinnamon
3 cups/260 g old-fashioned rolled oats
1 cup/140 g large golden raisins
½ cup/70 g large dried cranberries

Oh, Russell T. Davies. It's hard to believe you let the writers follow up something as amazing as The Empty Child/The Doctor Dances with a two part parody of contemporary reality TV.

Watching their lethal versions of Big Brother and The Weakest Link is a great reminder that Doctor Who is at its best when the episodes are timeless

If you want really appropriate foods for the lifelong reality show contestants of the new Satellite 5, go raid a gas station for whatever brightly colored packaged foods have the longest expiration date. If that sounds like a vile punishment, you can always chow down on these cookies instead. You can pretend they're a nutritious breakfast or a dessert treat, all while a Bad Wolf glares at you from the baking sheet.

To make these, beat your room temperature butter, brown sugar, and white sugar until they're as creamy and smooth as Captain Jack's bare chest. Now add in your eggs and vanilla, once more beating the mix until it gives you a saucy wink. Once your wet ingredients are well teased and ready for more, introduce them to the dry. Some people would put the flour, baking soda, salt, and cinnamon into a separate bowl and thoroughly mix them all together, but let's be honest. You're going to dump them all on top of the eggy sugar mix so you don't have to dirty a second bowl. I don't blame you. As long as you mix nice and thoroughly, everybody will play nicely together.

Once your mix looks irresistibly delicious, roughen it up a little by stirring in the rolled oats.

This is the point where you'd normally mix in all the raisins and cranberries, but these are Bad Wolf cookies. Instead, you're going to put the bowl in the freezer and walk away for 45 minutes. Gosh, that's just long enough to watch an episode.

When you come back, preheat your oven to 350F/178C. While it's warming up in anticipation, you get to make little wolf head cookies. If you have a wolf (or dog, or anything remotely closely) shaped cookie cutter, you're golden. If not, start with a nice circle, pinch off a muzzle at one end and pinch an ear at the other. It's okay if these look rough. If I lived in perpetual fear on Satellite 5 I'd be a shaky baker, too. Plant a cranberry where your wolf's eye should be. Outline the interior of its ear with raisins. If you have a neck area, you can always add a collar out of golden regular raisins, but this is a Bad Wolf, not a tame sheep dog, so don't stress.

Bake your cookies for 14-18 minutes, depending on how chewy (less time) or crispy (more baking) you prefer. Once they come out of the oven, let them cool at room temperature before shoveling them into your mouth. This is to let them firm up as well as to prevent you from burning your tongue. Your Bad Wolf cookies will keep at room temperature for 3-4 days, so feel free to make plenty in advance.

The Mad Dalek Emperor's All Seeing Eye (S1E13 - The Parting of the Ways)

6 small (3 oz/85 gram) boxes of purple Jell-O
6 cups/1.5 liters boiling water
6 cups/1.5 liters cold water
4 cups/1 liter vodka
¼ cup sweetened condensed milk or full fat coconut milk
1 hardboiled egg
1 round slice of black olive
4-6 drops red food coloring
plastic wrap

Am I the only one who looks at the unshelled Daleks and wonders where baby Daleks come from? Without their upended trash bin armor, Daleks look like meaty octopii who decided to climb out of the ocean and conquer the land out of sheer spite. Sometimes, like in this episode, they're shown floating in a crazy purple bath, cheerfully splashing their little tentacles to emphasize their madness. Other times, they look nearly deflated as they spat against the interior of their armor or glare from inside a life support tube.

In this case, the crazy Dalek emperor looks like a tentacled brain in a jar with one big, ugly, angry eye glaring out at the world. I could've concocted an exotic recipe using a whole baby octopus, but I've never been able to eat food that actually looks back at me. That left me with one obvious alternative. Jello shots. If you're having a bunch of Whovians over to watch some episodes, why not get drunk as a power mad Dalek by eating their tasty, tentacled brains?

You'll need a brain shaped refrigerator mold for this. If you don't already own one, you're welcome. This is your excuse. Anyone who owns this cookbook is going to have plenty of other excuses to use a brain shaped mold.

Start off by bringing six cups of water to a boil. Add in the six packages of purple (or a mix of 5 purple and 1 blue) Jell-O. Feel free to add a couple drops of red food coloring to make the whole thing more brain-like. Give it a good, hearty stir until the Jell-O powder is dissolved. Now toss in the 6 cups of cold water, 4 cups of Vodka, and ¼ cup of milk-like-substance. Veteran Jell-O lovers may notice the math doesn't quite add up here. Normally, it's 1 cup of boiling water to 2 cups of cold water. Ah, but when making Jell-O shots, if you want them to firm up properly, you need to skimp some on the water. Trust me. The coconut milk or sweetened condensed milk gives your mold a fleshy solidity so your Dalek emperor isn't weirdly transparent. If you can't drink milk, just use non dairy creamer. It'll be fine.

Coat your brain shaped mold with nonstick cooking spray and fill it with Jell-O. You should have a lot of Jell-O left. That's a good thing, because now we're going through the hassle of making tentacles. Get an 8x8 inch/20x20 centimeter square baking dish (for Americans, a brownie pan). Now bunch up your plastic wrap into rough tentacle shapes and put them in the bottom of the pan. Spritz them with non-stick coating, pour in the rest of your Jell-O mix, and put it in the fridge until it's nice and solid.

Meanwhile, peel your hardboiled egg and drop some red food coloring onto one end. Let it dribble down the side so you can get that angry, bloodshot eye effect.

Once everything cools, it's time to assemble your edible Dalek. Carefully upend the brain onto an oversized platter. You want room for tentaclly goodness. If it rips a little, relax. The Daleks all look like they're suffering from radiation poisoning. Yours just has some extra character. Extra crazy character.

Oh so carefully remove your tentacles from the brownie pan (if you want really long tentacles, you can scale things up by ⅓. Make two more packages of Jell-O, and add proportionately more water, milk-ish sludge, and most importantly, vodka. Instead of chilling it in a brownie pan, chill the tentacles in a cake or lasagna pan.)

Now curl the tentacles strategically around your Dalek emperor's brain. Once you're happy with their placement, carefully spoon out attachment areas so it looks like the tentacles are coming out of the flesh. Since this is Jell-O, you can use some of the stuff you just removed to patch up the holes where the tentacles connect. Finally, decide where you want your mad, bloodshot eye. Cut away a tiny bit of egg and shove the olive slice in as a pupil, or put a single edible googly eye in the hole. Use whatever you have around the house. Now scoop out about ⅔ of the egg's volume and carefully slide it into place. You want an angry, bulging Dalek eye, so make sure it's not flush with the surface. Finally, use a little of the Jell-O you just scooped out to create a makeshift eyelid area.

This makes a great alcoholic centerpiece for your Whovian gathering. If the whole Jell-O Brain isn't eaten, make sure you remove the eye before you put it in the fridge. You don't want to wake up hung over at 4 in the morning and see a half cannibalized Dalek glaring out at you from the back of your fridge.

SERIES 2: ROSE MEETS THE REGENERATION

The Doctor's Hand (S2E1 - The Christmas Invasion)

1 package hot dogs or beef brats
2 packages crescent roll dough
1 cup/200 g blanched, peeled almonds
cheddar cheese

I wanted to give you some kind of jellied hand floating in a blue liquid, but all my experiments in that direction were downright inedible. Instead, in honor of The Doctor's first new series regeneration, you're getting a super simple recipe that can be easily made by either children or drunks.

Cut your hot dogs in half length-wise. Four of them will make the fingers while the fifth will make the thumb and back of the hand. Pair up each hot dog sliver with an equal length of cheese. Now wrap the crescent roll dough around each one to make five fingers.

To make your hand look more organic, bunch up a roll of aluminum foil about the size of an orange. Drape one triangle of crescent dough over the aluminum foil to create the base of the hand. Arrange the fingers around the base of the hand. To make the thumb, simply stretch the fifth finger out in so it makes a straight line from the pinky to the forefinger. If you don't have enough extra thumb sticking out, add a little more hot dog near the pinky.

Put another triangle of crescent dough on top and start pinching it into place to seal up your hand. Otherwise, you'll have flesh sticking out of the edges. That's great for a zombie food, but this is The Doctor.

Once your dough is sealed and hand shaped, you can add a blanched almond to the tip of each finger as a fingernail. To be honest, no matter how hard I push them in, mine frequently fall out while the dough bakes. It's a nice effect when you can pull it off, but don't stress over it.

You should have enough supplies to make two hands. We'll ignore the fact that the doctor only had one hand cut off while defending the earth in his pajamas.

Bake the hands at 350F/178C for 14-16 minutes, or until golden brown and puffy. If they're still too white, continue cooking, checking every 2 minutes for doneness.

Let the hands cool for about 10 minutes. Serve them in the middle of a platter full of Satsuma's (or Clementine's, or any other small oranges) and small apples. Alternately, you can create an atmosphere more reminiscent of Captain Jack's Doctor Detector by piling the hand onto a platter of fresh, dry blueberries or blackberries. If you go that way, surround your hand with a wide arrow made of orange wedges and have fun pointing it in the direction of anyone cosplaying the tenth Doctor.

New Earth Apple Grass Cocktail (S2E2 - New Earth)

2 shots/90 ml lemon-lime soda
2 shots/90 ml clear apple juice
1 shot/45 ml vodka
½ shot/23 ml peach schnapps
½ shot/23 ml blue curacao
ice

New (to the 11th power) New York held a lot of recipe temptations, but there's something so heartwarming about Rose Tyler's excitement at the new ground beneath her feet during her first trip to New Earth. Drink a couple of these apple grass scented cocktails and you won't blink twice at cat faced nuns tending a futuristic hospital.

The apple juice gives this the right aroma for apple grass while the peach schnapps and blue curaco combine to give it the grassy color. The lemon-lime soda gives it a clean finish.

Mix the apple juice, vodka, peach schnapps and blue curacao in a cocktail shaker along with a handful of ice. Pound it like you're a force grown clone contemplating what might happen now that his once thin mistress lives in a fleshy mortal body.

Strain the result into a lowball glass and add a few ice cubes. Top it off with the lemon-lime soda and mix gently. Garnish the glass with a lime wedge. Drink enough of these and you won't care how the nurses achieve their miracle cures.

Queen Victoria's Nightcap (S2E3 - Tooth and Claw)

1 cup/235 ml Claret wine
1 shot/45 ml single malt whiskey

As the owners of Torchwood House could vouch, a visit from Queen Victoria was more of a nightmare than an honor. It wasn't unusual for her hosts to spend up to 70,000 pounds sterling on food and drink during one of her visits, during which they were expected to make her nine course meals with up to 30 different dishes.

Sadly, It's hard to keep up with demands like that when your manor is overrun with werewolves. The best you can do is hang some mistletoe garlands to keep the supernatural at bay while throwing back a couple of fortifying glasses of Queen Victoria's favorite tipple - a glass of Claret fortified with a shot of single malt whiskey. Yes, really. She must've had an iron liver.

I can't actually recommend this drink. I'm not a huge fan of Claret, and honestly, pouring good whiskey into bad wine seems like a crime against alcohol. However, if you want an authentic taste of the period, it's well worth trying. Once.

Deffry Vale School Chips with Krillitane Oil (S2E4 - School Reunion)

Baked Potatoes:
2 russet/jacket potatoes
4 tbsp/60 ml olive oil
1 tsp/5 g salt
1 tsp/5 g pepper
1 tsp/5 g garlic powder

Krillitane Oil:
4 tbsp/60 g mayonnaise
1 tsp/5 g dijon mustard
1 tsp/5 g curry powder
2 garlic cloves, minced
1 green apple, peeled and cored
¼ yellow onion
½ tsp/2.5 g salt
6-10 drops green food coloring.

When Anthony Stewart Head is in charge of your school, it's reasonable to expect a combination of fatherly lectures, world changing fights, and singing. This episode delivers one of those three things, and sadly, it's not the singing.

Let's clear up a little terminology first. What UK readers call chips, American readers call steak fries, or at perhaps thick cut French fries. To make it even more exciting, what American readers call chips UK readers would call crisps. At least everyone is still talking about potatoes.

Since Doctor Who is the UK's gift to the rest of the world, we're following their nomenclature. The Deffry Vale School chips are delicious, thick cut potato wedges served in an addictive sauce.

Let's be honest. You're going to pick up some chips from a shop (if you're in the UK) or a frozen bag of steak fries (in the US) before adding green dye to some catsup. I know it, you know it. However, since this is a cookbook, we'll maintain the adorable pretense that you're actually going to cook instead of taking the easy route.

The Krillitane would prefer you to eat deep fried chips, rich in delicious, brain enriching calories. However, since most people these days don't own deep fryers and your average middle class westerner is probably on a diet, we'll go with some nice baked chips instead. The dramatic part of this recipe is the Krillitane Oil.

To make the chips, start by preheating your oven to 425F/220C. While it warms up, scrub and peel some potatoes then cut them into long, wide rectangles. In a separate bowl, mix your olive oil, salt, pepper, and garlic powder. Coat a baking sheet with aluminum foil and heavily spritz it with non-stick spray. Dump the peeled, cut potatoes into the olive oil mix and gently toss everything together until the potatoes are well coated in oil and spices. Spread the coated potatoes into a single layer on your baking sheet.

Bake your potatoes for 25-30 minutes, turning once in the middle for maximum crispness. They won't be exactly the same as deep fried chips, but they'll only have half the calories and won't leave your home smelling like fried food.

While the potatoes are baking, mix up your delicious Krillitane Oil. Put the onion, apple, and garlic into a blender or food processor and let it whir away until you have a nice paste. Next, add the mayonnaise, mustard, salt, and six drops of food coloring. Let it whiz away some more. If the color isn't green enough for you, add more food coloring and process the blend some more. You should end up with a strong, sweet, curry flavored dip for your baked chips. They won't give you miraculous math powers, but they will make you grateful you no longer have to eat school lunches.

Fair warning: if you decide to just add some green dye to regular old red catsup, you'll end up with a dark green-brown paste with red highlights, somewhat reminiscent of a blood clot. While that can be cool in other contexts, you might be better off just making the Krillitane Oil dip from scratch.

The Doctor's Accidental Banana Daiquiri (S2E5 - The Girl in the Fireplace)

1 cup/110 g of crushed ice
1 banana
1 shot/45 ml of light rum
1 shot/45 ml of Cointreau
juice of ½ lime
2 tsp/10 g sugar
1 cherry

Always bring a banana to a party - especially if that party is in 18th century France. If you're The Doctor, you might use it to accidentally invent a banana daiquiri while partying with the future Madame du Pompadour.

Since your kitchen isn't limited to futuristic clockwork, simply put everything but the cherry into a nice, modern blender. Pulse it on slow for five seconds, give it a good stir, then crank it up to high and let it whiz away until your drink thickens up nicely. Yes, it's really that simple. No wonder he was able to invent one by accident. I expect he used one of the clockwork's innards as a blender after stealing its wig and coat.

In honor of the French, pour your banana daiquiri into a champagne glass and top it with a cherry.

Cybus Brain Cleansing Cocktail (S2E6 - Rise of the Cybermen)

3 shots/135 ml ginger beer
1 shot/45 ml vanilla vodka
1 shot/45 ml hazelnut liqueur
½ shot/23 ml butterscotch schnapps
thick grenadine syrup
aluminum foil ball

Between Jackie Tyler's birthday party and the invasion of the Cybermen, any survivors in Pete Tyler's alternate Earth would probably want a good brain cleansing to help them forget.

Pour some grenadine syrup into a saucer. Carefully dip the rim of your martini glass into the syrup so you have a nice bloody red line. Drop a quarter sized aluminum foil ball into the glass. You want it to be just large enough no one will swallow it by accident.

Fill a cocktail shaker with ice. Add the vanilla vodka, hazelnut liqueur, and butterscotch schnapps. Pound it like you're futily beating against a Cyberman's chest plate before you're carved into parts.

Carefully strain in the contents of the shaker. Top that off with the ginger beer. You should now have a tasty drink that looks like you carved open a skull and found nothing but metal inside.

The first time I made this, I tried dropping some edible ball bearings into the glass. The contents turned an angry brown and all the dye instantly fizzed off and a somewhat extended, slightly volcanic effect. I didn't end up with cool looking but harmless metal parts in my drink, but for a couple of minutes, it looked wildly dramatic. Sure, you can achieve the same effect with pop rocks, but the ball bearings didn't significantly impact the flavor of the drink. Use this knowledge wisely.

White Chocolate Cyberman Heads (S2E7 - The Age of Steel)

12 large strawberries
6 oz/170 g white melting chocolate
6 oz/170 g dark melting chocolate (optional)
black icing pen
large metal paper clips (optional)
edible silver spray paint (optional)

The first time I realized a white chocolate dipped strawberry looks like a Cybeman's head, I giggled like the voices that whisper messages via my dental fillings had just given me next week's lottery numbers. Those simplified faces make this a delightfully easy, instantly recognizable dessert. Making your own is also a heck of a lot cheaper than buying chocolate dipped strawberries and drawing faces on them. Honest.

This recipe will require a trip to your local craft store..

There, you'll find all kinds of melting chocolate, edible spray paint, precision sizes of icing pens, and all the tools needed to bake the amazing cakes that are so trendy these days Luckily, you can use these for the far simpler process of decorating Cyberman heads.

Most people will tell you to put the melting chocolate in the top part of a double boiler and stir slowly and constantly until you reach your desired texture. However, my local craft store has a huge aisle of microwavable melting chocolate. If you don't have a double boiler, this stuff is magic. Just put it in a microwave safe glass bowl, nuke it for a few seconds, massage the bag, nuke some more, and within minutes, those of you who don't own double boilers can achieve the same effect. Modernity is awesome.

However you choose to do it, melt your chocolate. You want to get it just runny enough to stick to your strawberries. Too hot and it'll burn, which results in all kinds of nastiness.

Cover a baking sheet with aluminum foil or wax paper then spritz it with nonstick spray. Hold your strawberries by the green stem and dip them in your melted chocolate. Roll them around a little to make sure you have good coverage. Lay each strawberry gently on your baking sheet to cool.

Flavor-wise, I personally like to dip my strawberries in a thick layer of dark chocolate first, let them cool, then dip them in white chocolate to finish. If you're a big white chocolate fan, feel free to just dunk them in the white stuff.

Regardless of what's underneath, once they have a nice, white surface, gently draw on a circle for the eyes. If you're good at drawing, you can use a toothpick to tug some of the icing down in the corner of each eye to make the fake tear effect on our sad Cybermen. Draw a diagonal line under each eye for the cheekbones, then a straight line down to the mouth. For the mouth, just draw a simple rectangular box. Connect up your top lines so they form a bridge over the eyes.

You can try to finish the CyberBerry by unfolding a metal paper clip and rearranging it into the shape of the squared head antenna. In theory, you should be able to just plug the paperclip into each side of your Cyberman's head. In reality, paperclips are a lot sturdier than I anticipated. You're likely to squish a lot of berries. Worse yet, the antannae have an annoying habit of refusing to stay in position. Feel free to try. If you can pull it off, it looks fantastic. If you can't, don't stress. The painted berries look great.

If you're feeling extra schmancy, after your chocolate dries but before you decorate the face, you can spray the berries with edible silver paint. I can never decide which effect I like better. People giggle more at the silver berries, but they're also less likely to eat them. If you want to have tasty strawberries left after your party, go for the paint. If you made too many and just need to get rid of them all, leave them unpainted. Either way, you'll still get compliments for their cuteness.

Coronation Chicken (S2E8 - The Idiot's Lantern)

2 baked chickens
1 tbsp/15 ml cooking oil
4 tbsp/60 g onions, chopped
2 tsp/10 g curry powder
1 tsp/5 g tomato paste
1/2 cup/110 ml red wine
¼ cup/60 ml water
1 bay leaf
2 lemons
6 dried apricots
2 cups/450 g mayonnaise
3 tbsp/45 ml whipping cream
1 tsp/5 g sugar
1 tsp/5 g fresh ground black pepper
1 tsp/5 g salt
paprika and parsley for garnish

One of the best things about Doctor Who is the fact that it provides you with a glimpse into recent history. For the UK target audience, their parents or grandparents lived through this time. For Americans and other foreign creatures, wartime Britain is as alien as the Ood.

So keep in mind, World War II was horrible in subtle ways as well as the big scary ones. People stoically suffered through years of food rationing and deprivation almost impossible to imagine in an era of 24 hour McDonald's. When they were allowed to loosen their belts just a little bit to celebrate the coronation of a new queen, this is what they ate.

You don't have to be a living wire hiding in a television signal to appreciate the sheer caloric richness of this dish, or how remarkable so much cream and fat must have tasted after so many years of rations and austerity.

First, bake your chickens. Since you're living in the 21st century, you can always pick up a pair of pre-cooked rotisserie chickens from your local grocery store. Once the chickens are cooked and cool, pick off all the meat. Toss everything else in a crockpot with an unpeeled quartered onion, a couple bay leaves, and a couple sticks each of celery and carrots. Fill it up with water, set it to low, and leave it alone for the next eight hours. You don't need this for the recipe, but if you have a couple of chicken carcasses lying around, you might as well make fresh broth out of them. It's dirt simple, freezes beautifully, and is more delicious than anything you'll get out of a box. In 8-12 hours, strain out the solids and enjoy your liquid gold.

Now for your coronation chicken.

Add your oil and onions to a medium saucepan. Cook the onions until they're softened but not yet brown. Add the curry powder, tomato puree, wine, water, bay leaf, and a healthy squeeze from half a lemon. Simmer, uncovered, for 5-10 minutes, then strain. Leave it to cool. Meanwhile, put the apricots into another pan and add just enough water to cover them. Simmer the apricots until they're tender enough to fall apart.

In a big bowl, mix your mayonnaise, simmered apricots, and onion mix. Add the sugar, salt, and black pepper. In yet another bowl, get out your blender and whip your cream until it magically transforms from a liquid to a solid. Once it's nice and firm, gently fold it in with the mayonnaise mix.

Now it's finally time to add all that shredded chicken. This was meant to be a rich dish, worthy of a queen. Mix everything until the chicken is downright sloppy with sauce. Arrange it neatly in a serving dish, then garnish the edges with neatly sliced lemon rounds and sprinkle your choice of paprika or parsley in the middle. Being an American, I think it tastes nice when topped with coleslaw and served in a tortilla, but you're welcome to just ladle it onto a plate and soak up the extra sauce with bread.

Chicken and Ood Soup (S2E9 - The Impossible Planet)

1 small roast chicken
4 carrots
2 stalks celery
1 onion
4 large cloves of garlic
1 tsp/5 g kosher salt
1 cup/240 g matzoh meal
4 eggs
4 tsp/60 g fat (olive oil or schmaltz, melted chicken fat)
1 tsp/5 g salt
4 tbsp/60 ml sparkling tonic water
1 tsp/5 g garlic powder
1 tsp/5 g onion powder

Hello, Ood. your formal suits and sugared licorice stick mouths completely make up for the bad CGI asteroid base seen from space.

I love this dish so much. It's easier than you would expect from the length of the ingredients list. More importantly, it always, without fail, makes Whovians laugh. As if that's not enough to endorse it, this dish has the added benefit of tasting pretty darn good. You're basically going to make a cup of deconstructed matzoh ball soup that looks like an Ood staring back at you from a teacup.

Let's start with the soup itself. It doesn't matter if you made a chicken for dinner a couple days ago or if you picked up one of the cheap pre-cooked whole rotisserie chickens available in nearly every grocery deli. You want to carefully remove as much of the meat from the bones as possible. Try to keep the breast meat intact. You're going to need that later. You can also just buy some plain chicken breasts and grill them up, but they'll be less juicy, more expensive, and won't leave you with a carcass when you're done.

You want the carcass to make broth. Honest. Once you've removed the breasts, put the rest of your chicken in a crockpot and fill it with enough water to completely submerge the carcass. Peel your onion, cut it into quarters, and toss it in. If you're in an angry mood, you can simply use your fists to break the carrots and celery before throwing them in. Heck, go ahead and take a hammer to the peeled garlic cloves to show them who's boss. You might want to throw in a bay leaf and a couple of cloves. Finish it all with a teaspoon of kosher salt. Now put the lid on, turn the crockpot down to low, and walk away. Eight hours later (when you come home from work, for example, or first thing the next morning) you'll have a delicious broth that will make you swear off the stuff that comes in boxes. The skin and bones are full of tasty fats and trapped flavor which you've now released so it will do your bidding.

Strain away the solids. If your stock has some pesky floating bits, put a couple layers of cheesecloth over a strainer and pour it through again.

Put the broth into a large stock pot. If you have less than 8 cups/2 liters, add water until you reach the 8 cup/2 liter point. If you have more, save it for use in other recipes. You're going to be drinking this stuff later, so feel free to add extra salt, pepper, or herbs to your liking.

Now for the matzoh balls. The easiest thing to do is just buy a boxed mix and follow the directions. Sure, they'll taste better made from scratch, but most of your guests won't know the difference. I normally like a little dill in mine, but since these make up the face of your Ood, you don't want any stray flecks of herbs making it look like your Ood has a skin condition.

Mix all the dry ingredients in one bowl. Next, mix the wet ingredients in another bowl. I know you want to dump them all in a single bowl and call it a day, but if you over-mix the batter, your matzoh balls will turn out tough and unpleasant. Once you've mixed your wet and dry ingredients separately, quickly introduce them to one another. Like a good hostess, engage in a minimum of forced mingling then get out of the way so they can get to know one another. Put the matzoh ball dough in the fridge for an hour (or up to 4) and let the chemical composition of your dumplings work its magic in privacy.

This is a good time to prepare the rest of your soup. Remember that chicken breast meat? You're going to julienne it. Cut the meat into long, thin, tentacle-like strips, going against the grain. You should have a nice, big pile of chicken meat. Dust it lightly with paprika to give your chicken tentacles a reddish color. (If you prefer, you can use sumac for a mild Persian flavor or chili powder if you want a southwestern kick.)You also want to cut your roasted red bell pepper strips into almond shaped eyes. They should be just big enough to fit half an olive as the pupil.

To make your matzoh balls, start by bringing a large pot of water to a boil. Use a large spoon or melon baller to gently scoop out 2-3 inch wide balls. Handle them as little as possible while shaping them, then drop the balls into the boiling water. Once all the balls are in the water, wait for them to rise to the top. Now, turn the heat down to a modest simmer, put the lid on the pot, and let the balls cook for 40 minutes.

I know you'll want to look, but resist the temptation. Leave the lid. Don't look. Don't even think about stirring the matzoh balls. After 40 minutes, they will have transformed into fluffy dough balls you can carefully lift out of the water with a slotted spoon. Mess with them and they'll turn into angry, rubbery lumps.

Now for the fun part.

Get a nice, large teacup and saucer. Put a matzoh ball into the teacup and gently, carefully, fill it 2/3 of the way up with your homemade soup stock. Grab a few of those chicken tentacles you carved up earlier and arrange them so they're spilling from the Ood's "mouth," so they cascade over the edge of the teacup. You can outline the mouth with a thin line of roasted red bell pepper strip if you'd like. Apply the pre-cut roasted red bell pepper eyes you made earlier, being careful not to poke your Ood too hard. You don't want to dislodge the mouth tentacles. Complete the eyes by laying the olive pupils in place.

For added effect, you'll want to finish the Ood with a clear tendril connecting it to a brain. If you like Asian food, I recommend picking up some thick rice noodles for the tendril and some red bean paste filled glutinous rice balls for the external brain itself. The look is fantastic, and they're not hard to prepare according to package directions. If you don't have a convenient Asian grocery, you can always buy some pre-made coconut macaroons or the round, powdered sugar coated cookie of your choice and attach it to the Ood with a long strand of string cheese, a clear bendy straw, or even a tube made from rolled up plastic wrap. In a pinch, just use some string cheese and a hard boiled egg.

If you're having a sit down Doctor Who themed meal, this makes an incredible presentation dish. People are boggled when they see an Ood face staring up at them from their place setting. Once they've admired the presentation, just shove the chicken strips into the tea cup and eat it like a normal bowl of soup. If your guests are confused about how to eat matzoh ball soup, just tell them it's a Whovian cup of chicken and dumplings. You'll be amazed how fast they figure it out.

In addition to the sheer, glorious look, this recipe also offers one of your best values per dollar (or pound). A whole chicken (even the fully cooked rotisserie version) is cheaper than picking up a boneless, skinless breast for everyone. Either a box of matzoh ball soup mix or ingredients from scratch are equally inexpensive. Sure, it takes time, but I can make servings for 12 with a big bowl of leftover soup for less than $10. You get an incredible dish for about twice the cost of ramen. If you're only going to try one time-consuming recipe from this entire book, this should be the one. You won't regret it.

Black Hole Mezze (S2E10 - The Satan Pit)

raisins
black mission figs
blueberries
blackberries
hardboiled eggs
blue corn chips
corn and black bean salsa
lemon or orange peel

If you're trapped on a ship full of Ood possessed by Satan, you might need a couple of snacks before you desperately try to escape.

One of the nice things about this is you can easily use it for any Whovian starscape. In fact, if you're particularly artistic, you can even use the same ingredients as the base of a Starry Night scene in honor of Vincent Van Gogh meeting The Doctor in a couple of seasons.

If you have a couple of differently sized metal burner bibs, put the smaller one inside the larger. Weight down the space in between with some large metal nuts (available at any hardware store). This gives you the look of a porthole into space.

If you're not into the porthole look, simply grab a white plate (for contrast) or a baking sheet (if you're feeding a lot of people.)

Spread a layer of raisins as the base blackness of space. Create some blue-black contrast with blueberries or blackberries. Black mission figs, arranged in a nice circle, give the impression of a black hole. You can crumble the egg yolk around the black hole(s) and maybe sprinkle a little bit in the middle to represent the fiery collapse. Create stars by mincing your egg whites and sprinkling them into anything from constellations to galaxies over the fruity darkness of space. If you want to keep the plate vegan, just leave out the egg.

Meanwhile, on an adjacent porthole or plate, create a menacing pit of corn and black bean salsa then surround it with an explosion of blue corn chips. You get your sweets, your salts, your crunchies, and a dash of protein all while satisfying a hunger that stems from the dawn of time. Or lunch.

L.I.N.D.A.'s Tardis Wellington (S2E11 - Love and Monsters)

Duxelles:
1 lb/455 g white button mushrooms
2 small onions, peeled and roughly chopped
4 cloves garlic, peeled and roughly chopped
2 sprigs fresh thyme, leaves only
4 tbsp/60 g butter
1 tsp/5 g fresh ground black pepper
½ tsp/2.5 g kosher salt

Beef:
2 lb/900 g sirloin tip roast, carefully trimmed of all fat
1 lb/450 g puff pastry, thawed if using frozen
2 tbsp/60g dijon mustard
2 large eggs, lightly beaten
kosher salt and freshly ground black pepper

This is a great recipe for getting your mates get together for a little Electric Light Orchestra jam sessions and alien spotting. Don't be intimidated by the "Wellington" name. This is actually easier to make than most people think. The key is quality ingredients. Yes, it is a little bit of a hassle, but your friends will be talking about it for ages.

You can use beef tenderloin in this recipe, but you won't end up with the flatter, more square shape you want in a Tardis shaped meat pie. Instead, go for a nice, thick sirloin tip roast. They're tender enough some people call the sirloin tip a "poor man's prime rib." Most cuts also happen to be just the right shape and texture for this recipe. Fair warning: don't use a cheap, tough roast. You'll end up with an inedible lump. Cheap cuts of meat need to be cooked slowly for long periods of time before they soften up. Just this once, go for the good stuff. If you can't find any sirloin tip roast, ask your butcher what he'd substitute in a big, flat Wellington. Most of them will be totally relieved someone still cares about meat. If he stares at you blankly, it's time to find a new grocery store.

Once you're ready to make your Tardis Wellington, take your frozen puff pastry out of the freezer and let it thaw at room temperature. This takes a few hours, so you're best off just putting the box in the fridge to thaw slowly the night before

When picking your sirloin tip roast, try to find one that's already got as much rectangular potential as possible. You'll probably have to cut it down a little to make sure it's properly Tardis shaped. Luckily, the remains can either be grilled outside as steaks or turned into kabobs if they're odd sizes. Make sure to carefully trim all visible fat from your sirloin tip roast then carve it into a nice rectangle that weighs around 2 pounds.

Preheat your oven to 400F/205C. When it's good and hot, bake your rectangle of roast for 20-25 minutes, or until the interior temperature reaches 130F/55C. Don't leave it in too long. It'll be back in the oven after being covered in puff pastry. You bake it in two steps like this to make sure the meat is properly done without burning the puff pastry.

While the meat is roasting, it's time to make the duxelles. That's just a fancy term for the mushroom and shallot topping that gets baked inside the crust. Melt your butter in a skillet over medium heat. If you enjoy chopping vegetables, mince up your mushrooms, onions, and garlic. If you consider it a chore, throw them all in a food processor, along with the fresh thyme, and pulse it a few times until you end up with a nice vegetable mince. Don't let it run too long or else you'll end up with a vegetable paste.

Toss your veggie mix into your melted butter and cook it all for about eight to ten minutes. It should be gloriously aromatic. Finish the mix with your salt and pepper, cook for another minute or so, then set it aside to cool.

It may seem counter intuitive, but once the meat and veggies are ready, you want to put them in the fridge to cool down a bit. This is so they don't soak through the puff pastry and thereby ruin the crust. Leave them be for an hour or so while you watch another episode of Doctor Who.

When you come back, it's time for the fun part.

Unfold your puff pastry. It should be large enough to wrap your entire roast. (If in doubt, buy two boxes of puff pastry dough. This isn't the place to skimp.) Now carefully cut an inch or so off one of the shorter edges so you have a line of thin scraps. You'll be using these to decorate the top into a Tardis shape.

Carefully pat your roast dry with some paper towels.

Spread your duxelles out in the middle of your puff pastry. You want to make a rectangle of it a little smaller than your meat. Now carefully spread a generous amount of dijon mustard over one side of your meat and put it mustard side down on top of the duxelles. Once the meat is in place, oh so carefully fold in the edges of the puff pastry so they overlap. You want to essentially wrap your meat in the puff pastry as though it's an edible Christmas present. Feel free to cut away any extra pastry that doesn't fit.

Now for the hard part. Carefully flip the whole thing over so it's seam side down in a pre-buttered pan. This gives you a nice, smooth surface for the rectangular top of your Tardis.

If you squint, you can see the potential within, but it doesn't really look like a Tardis. Not yet. You want to use the puff pastry scraps to finish off the effect. Start by cutting strips to make a half inch wide rectangle around the top of the roast. Position this a good inch/2.5 cm inwards from the edges. Otherwise, you risk having your decorations simply fall off the sides when the puff pastry expands during baking. I speak from experience. Once your border is in place, add another strip down the middle, lengthwise. Now add three evenly spaced strips across the width to represent the upper windows, the warning plaque, and the bottom of the doors. Cut a small circle of pastry and put it in the second box on the right. Cut a little square of puff pastry and put it in the second box on the left. If you have enough puff pastry left, make a thin cross (to represent window panes) in each of the top two boxes. Stop and admire for a moment. It's lovely.

To make sure it comes out of the oven a beautiful golden brown, beat your eggs until they're slightly frothy. Use a pastry brush to coat the entire exterior of your puff pastry. Lightly sprinkle the whole thing with kosher salt. Add a little extra salt to the middle left box that represents the plaque so it'll be nice and sparkly.

Now pop the whole thing in a 400F/205C oven and bake it for 25-35 minutes, depending on your preferred level of doneness. Feel free to sneak a meat thermometer into the side to check the temperature. You want it about 130F/55C (140/60C if you prefer your roast closer to medium well.) If your roast isn't done enough, cover the top with aluminum foil and cook for another 5-7 minutes. Final cooking time has as much to do with the thickness of your roast as the weight. The thinner the meat, the faster it cooks.

If you're feeling extra fancy, once your Tardis is finished baking, you can fill the top two windows with either some carefully carved egg whites or some pale white cheese, and perhaps even create some shadows in each of the boxes using either a spread made from diced black olives or some Japanese nori (seaweed paper used to make sushi.)

A good roast needs at least 20 minutes to cool before serving. Otherwise, you'll lose all the delicious juiciness inside. Luckily, this gives you plenty of time for guests to admire your hard work. When you're ready to serve it, simply cut the Tardis into 1-2 inch/2.5 - 5 centimeter thick slices.

If you desperately want a Tardis on the table but you're intimidated by the idea of a fancy roast, don't despair. There's a perfectly good cheater's option that will get you 80% of the look for a fraction of the effort.

Get yourself a couple rolls of unperforated crescent dough at the grocery store. Sure, you can also use pizza dough, but the crescents are easier to work with and create a more consistent final result. Now, make whatever casserole you normally enjoy. Chicken pot pie works a treat, as does a tamale pie, or even a shepherd's pie. Prep your casserole in the usual fashion, spread a nice, flat layer of crescent dough on top, then follow the same procedure using dough scraps to create the details. You can probably throw this crust together in ten minutes, and that's only if you take some time on the windows. Bake your casserole with the Tardis crust on top and enjoy the envy and admiration of your friends.

Whatever sort of meaty goodness you make, it's best served with some Electric Light Orchestra Karaoke and the company of your favorite people whose lives have been touched by The Doctor.

2012 Olympic Shortbread Medallions (S2E12 - Fear Her)

¾ lb/170 g unsalted butter
1 cup/200 g granulated sugar
1 tsp/5 ml pure vanilla extract
3 1/2 cups/225 g all-purpose flour
1/4 tsp/1 g kosher salt
icing
colored sugar
colored ribbon

I was tempted to offer you a tooth crunchingly horrible dessert since The Doctor loves cake with ball bearings you can eat. However, in honor of the sad, alternate world where London suffered from some sort of bizarre austerity Olympics instead of the pop culture extravaganza of our world's 2012 opening ceremonies, I give you these Olympic Medals. If you're not feeling the Olympic love, you can always stencil on the Seal of Rassilon instead. Either way, wear them proudly around your neck.

Preheat your oven to 350F/178C. While the oven is heating, cream together your butter and sugar. Mix in your vanilla. If you're a good person, you'll mix your flour and salt in another bowl, but we both know you're just going to dump the dry ingredients in the same bowl with your deliciously buttery sugar. It'll be alright. Just mix it up as best you can.

Once the dough is a nice, consistent solid, shape it into a ball full of cookie potential and put it in the fridge for 30 minutes. That's almost enough time to watch an episode. You're entirely forgiven if you actually come back 45 minutes later.

Dust your working surface with a little flour. Roll the dough out until it's only about ¾ of an inch/2 cm thick. Use a round cookie cutter to cut out your medallions. Since you want to be able to hang them from a ribbon, use a screwdriver or the end of an ink pen to cut a neat round hole at one end.

Bake your cookie medallions on an ungreased baking sheet for 20 to 25 minutes, or until the edges just start to brown.

Let the cookies cool down to room temperature before you decorate them. If you want to host your own Whovian Olympics, decorate the cookies with a nice yellow lemony icing for gold, a white cream cheese icing for silver, and a caramel colored icing for bronze. Use icing to write 1, 2, and 3 on the representative cookies.

Alternately, if you all want to be Time Lords, print out a Seal of Rassilon and use an exacto knife to carefully cut it into a stencil. Lightly ice the cookies, lay the stencil in place, then dust the top with colored sugar. Carefully peel off the stencil.

Whichever type of cookie you make, thread the hole with a long string of colored ribbon so people can wear their trophies around their neck, at least, until they're ready for a snack.

Cyberman Ghosts (S2E13 - Army of Ghosts)

2 cups/270 g sushi rice
2 tbsp/30 ml sweetened sushi rice vinegar (available in the
same aisle as the rice)
2 sheets nori
6 oz/170 g sushi grade tuna
4 tbsp/60 g mayonnaise
1 tsp/5 ml sesame oil
1 tsp/5 ml Sriracha or other Asian hot sauce
1 tsp/5 ml sweetened rice wine vinegar
1 red bell pepper (optional)
aluminum foil
small frozen blueberries

We all know that inside every Cyberman is the brain of a
once living human being. Likewise, these sushi balls are
stuffed with something deliciously red and bloody.

You can either decorate these sushi rice balls with full Cyberman armor or leave them the amorphous "ghosts" seen in the episode.
Vegetarians are welcome to substitute red bell peppers for the tuna. (Tomato would have a better color and consistency, but it's so
wet it would ruin the sushi.)

Cook your sushi rice according to package directions. I have a rice cooker. If you make much rice at home, these things are
amazingly easy to use, dirt cheap to buy, and produce nearly miraculous results. I can't recommend them enough.

While your rice is cooking, dice your sushi grade tuna into small pieces. Mix the mayo, sesame oil, Sriracha, and one teaspoon of
sweetened rice vinegar. Feel free to add a little hot chili oil if that's too mild for you. Mix in your minced tuna. This is now your
Cyberman's brain.

If you're a vegetarian, feel free to substitute a minced red bell pepper for the tuna. It won't taste the same, but isn't that the point?
You still get a tasty red brain explosion, only yours has a little crunch to it.

However you make your rice, once it's finished, douse it with 2 tablespoons of sweetened rice wine vinegar. I know fancy home
sushi chefs will mix rice wine vinegar with sugar and salt to make their own, but honestly, I cut that out when no one was able to
tell the difference between my home mix and the bottled stuff. Just make sure the pre-made brand you buy uses actual sugar instead
of high fructose corn syrup.

Now for the fun part. Grab a small handful of rice and pack it nice and tight. You're making a Cyberman's head. Hollow it out a
little and stuff some of your tuna or red bell pepper brains inside. Seal the head closed with some more rice. You can leave it
amorphous, like the ghosts in this episode. If you like sculpting, go ahead and give it some features then decorate the surface with
bits of Nori or an icing pen to make the Cyberman face. When you're done, bend some metal paperclips into the familiar
rectangular head antenna and stuff those in around where your cyberman should have ears. Finish them off with two small frozen
blueberries for the eyes.

Fishy Daleks (S2E14 - Doomsday)

6 triangular frozen fish filets
Pocky Sticks
catsup
mustard
cotton swabs
tartar sauce

There's something fishy about a giant cosmic egg full of Daleks.

If you're intimidated by the thought of making sushi brains or a Tardis Wellington, this is a cheap, simple alternative you can whip up with zero cooking skill. It also happens to give you nicely decorated raw ingredients for the Fish Fingers and Custard Tacos in Chapter 7.

Those rhombus shaped fish filets already look suspiciously like Daleks. All they need is a little extra decoration and you can nickname them Sec, Thay, Caan, and Jast.

Bake the fish filets according to package directions. Once they're crispy and edible, use the mustard to draw armor lines on the body. Dot the body with your choice of catsup or tartar sauce armor eggs.

Shove a couple of broken Pocky sticks on one side and a snipped cotton swab on the other to represent the Dalek's arms. If you happen to have any olive slices, put one on your Dalek's head to represent the eyestalk.

Including baking time, you'll have these on the table in half an hour. If you're looking for something that's both a good Whovian in-joke and a variation from the endless fish fingers and custard spreads, this is a nice alternative. You can always meet the fish finger folks in the middle by putting out a tray of some of the savory fake custard alternatives you'll also find lurking in the last chapter.

SERIES THREE: SMITH AND JONES

Huon Particle Cocktail (S3E1 - The Runaway Bride)

3 shots/130 ml Champagne or sparkling wine
½ shot/22 ml clear raspberry liqueur
Fresh raspberries

This is a simple cocktail in honor of a complicated wedding. Poor Donna Noble. It's hard enough to lose your fiancé, but losing him to an impossibly giant cross between a spider and a crab could hurt any woman's ego. The best thing to do is drink it off and hope a madman in a blue box comes to rescue you.

Again.

Add half a shot of Chambord (or your favorite raspberry liqueur) to the bottom of a champagne flute. Top the flute off with champagne. Drop in 3-4 raspberries, to symbolize the Racnoss Empress. If you're feeling extra fancy (and you have cooperatively sturdy fruit) you can even garnish the glass with another raspberry.

This refreshing cocktail is best served at a festive occasion alongside a tray of dark pink crab legs artistically arranged to look like a spider.

Moon Cake Pops (S3E2 - Smith and Jones)

1 box of cake mix
1 tub of pre-made frosting
1 8 oz/220 g bag of white melting chocolate
1 tbsp/15 g butter
a handful of chocolate chips
powdered hot chocolate mix
long lollipop sticks or bamboo skewers
paintbrush
styrofoam block for display

If you've had a hard day of being abducted by giant walking rhinos, you deserve a nice commemorative dessert. Luckily, it's easy to make these cake pops look like tiny, edible moons.

You have a lot of good flavor choices here. If you want to make your cake interior look really moon-like, pick up a box of spice cake or carrot cake. Realistically, though, those aren't your favorite flavors. You're probably going to pick chocolate. I'm a big fan of lemon. Or strawberry. Or red velvet. Let's be honest, I'm just a big fan of cake. Whatever you pick, just get the corresponding icing.

Bake your cake according to the package directions. Once it's finished, resist the urge to stuff the warm cake directly into your face. If you're notorious for poor self control, bake an auxiliary backup cake. Once your primary Whovian cake is finished, let it cool down to room temperature. Now let your inner five year old run loose and rip that cake to shreds. Seriously. Tear into it with your fingers until you have nothing but a gorgeous mess of shredded cake goodness.

Meanwhile, soften the tub of icing in your microwave. Pour ¾ of it over the cake crumbles. If you use the whole tub of icing, your cake pops will end up too mushy. Resist the temptation. You want to moisten the cake and hold it together without making it unpalatabley gooey. Now really mix the cake and icing together until you have a solid cake paste.

Line a cookie sheet with aluminum foil and spritz it with nonstick spray. If you have a cookie scoop or melon baller, use that to scoop nicely shaped balls into your hands. Roll them around a little to get them as moon shaped as possible, then line them up on the cookie sheet. Your hands are about to get really goopy. Every half dozen or so, be prepared to go wash your hands (and maybe re-grease them with some spare butter to keep future cake balls from sticking.)

Once you're out of cake, put the tray of balls into your freezer for at least an hour. You want them to firm up so they'll play nicely with the icing. While the cake balls are chilling, pour your white melting chocolate into a large, microwave safe bowl. In the United States, you can find this at most craft stores, such as Michael's or Hobby Lobby. Cut 1 tablespoon/15 grams of butter into four small pieces and toss them in the bowl. While you're at it, toss in a couple chocolate chips. These don't add much flavor, but they do help turn the white chocolate more of a moon-like grey.

When your cake pops have firmed up, follow the package directions to melt the chocolate in the microwave. Alternately, you can melt the chocolate in a double boiler, but it takes a lot longer and requires you to have an actual double boiler. This recipe is for lazy people who want to look fancy, and we both know that means you don't own a whole lot of exotic pans. Now that your chocolate is melted, it's time for the fun part. Skewer each ball with a lollipop stick or actual bamboo kabob skewer. Dip it in the chocolate, roll it around a bit, and make sure the entire ball is nice and coated. Shove the skewers into a styrofoam block (which you can also pick up at the craft store) so the cake pop keeps it's moon shape.

Grease your fingers up with butter and poke little crater shapes into the moons. Once the icing has cooled, you can use the powdered hot chocolate mix and a paint brush to dust on shadows in the craters and give the moons a little more contrast and definition. Or you can drink the hot chocolate while admiring all your hard work making these miniature moons. I'm not going to judge.

Psst...these work equally well as "Day of the Moon" themed decorations.

Shakespearean Shooter Sandwich (S3E3 - The Shakespeare Code)

1 crusty round loaf of bread
2 lbs/910 g steak, preferably not too lean
1 lb/500 g mushrooms
½ lb/230 g leeks or onions
8 tbsp/75 g butter
2 tbsp/30 ml Worcestershire sauce
4 garlic cloves
3.5 oz/100 ml brandy or whiskey|
nor (optional)

That beard. That swagger. Oh, Shakespeare. You've never been so sexy.

If you slipped into the Tardis for Martha's first journey back in time, you could not only enjoy the only production of Shakespeare's "Love's Labour's Won," but also a hearty slice of what would later be called a Shooter's Sandwich. It's a sort of cheap cheater's version of a hearty meat pie made by people who didn't have access to an oven. One dense slice would keep you full for the duration of a four hour long performance. For you historians, this is technically an Edwardian recipe. However, food historians agree that by the time a recipe was written down, it had usually been in use and circulation for decades, so there are good odds you'd find this served at theaters like the Globe. Groundlings needed some hearty fare for a day of mocking actors and pretending to flirt with boys in dresses. This would've been perfect.

Start by slicing off the top quarter of your hearty round loaf. Scoop out about ⅔ of the interior. You can pull the interior apart and let the scraps dry in order to make homemade croutons. Thinly slice your mushrooms, garlic, and leeks or onions. Melt your butter in a skillet and toss in your vegetables. You want to sauté them over a medium high heat until they're reduced down to about half their previous bulk. Add the Worcestershire sauce and brandy or whiskey then give it a good stir. Let it continue to cook down while you prepare the steaks.

While your vegetables enjoy their drink, take a shot for yourself before rubbing your steaks down with a generous amount of salt and pepper. This part isn't entirely period, since pepper would be a bit pricy in Shakespeare's day, but in our modern, decadent era you can afford to live a little. Speaking of living a little, treat yourself to some nice, fatty ribeyes. If you use a really lean meat you'll end up with an unpleasantly dry, tough sandwich. You want something with some real substance in this manly sandwich.

Rub a tiny amount of butter into the bottom of a hot skillet and sear your steaks for a couple of minutes on each side. You want to keep them nice and juicy for the sandwich, so don't go overboard. Aim for medium rare to medium. While the steaks are still dripping and hot, tuck them into the hollowed out loaf of bread. You want to create a solid layer of meat across the bottom. If you're feeling fancy, you can now smear the steaks with some horseradish or mustard for extra flavor. When you're done, top the meat off with all your vegetables. Try to really cram them down inside. If you'd like, you can top the whole thing off with a thick layer of cheese.

Now put the lid back on your bread. It looks as innocent as a pretty young witch. You'd never imagine what's really inside. If you want to give it some extra flair, use an exacto knife to cut out a giant DW or Seal of Rassilon from the nori and put it over the middle of the bread lid.

Wrap the sandwich in waxed paper and tie it loosely with butcher's string. This is to keep everything in place so you don't end up with a sandwich that's all mushroom in one bite and all meat in the next. You need to keep it all in place because next, you're going to crush it as thoroughly as the tenth Doctor crushes Martha's heart. Flatten the wrapped sandwich under something heavy - the complete Yale Shakespeare is a good start. If you have bricks or cinderblocks lying about, you can pile them on top of a board. Put some real weight onto it. You're about to crush the sandwich down into a hearty mock pie.

Let the sandwich sit under the weights, unrefrigerated, for at least 6 hours, preferably overnight. The end result should be a fantastically dense, room temperature sandwich When you're ready to serve it, cut the sandwich into pie-like slices. A little goes a very long way. To add to the period feel, hire a cross dresser to serve it with apples and nuts.

Kitty Nurse Kibble (S3E4 - Gridlock)

3 cups/700 g rolled oats (not instant)
1 cup/200 g nuts and seeds
½ cup/120 g dried fruit
½ cup/100 ml dark honey
¼ cup/50 g unsweetened coconut flakes
1 tsp/5 g cinnamon
1 tbsp/15 ml vanilla

We're back on New Earth, where the Face of Boe is once more being tended by personal nun and part time pet kitty, Novice Hame.

In honor of the cars endlessly circling below, I humbly offer this anthropomorphized cat chow.

It packs densely, is shelf stable at room temperature for months, and is equally nutritious whether you're on an endless roadtrip or living with your head in the clouds.

Preheat your oven to 300F/150C. While the oven warms up, soften your honey in the microwave for 15-20 seconds. You don't want it to boil, but you do want to get it a little bit runny. Mix in the vanilla and cinnamon. Once those are well blended, add your oats, coconut flakes, and nuts or seeds. Personally, I like pepitas and peanuts, but feel free to use sunflower seeds, flax seeds, pecans, walnuts, almonds, or whatever crunchy bits suit you.

I usually start this process by coating a large plastic spoon in olive oil (so the mix won't stick to the spoon) and really putting my elbow into it, but I still end up with some bits too dry and others too soggy. I recommend skipping this well intentioned but ultimately delusional step. Just rub your hands down with some oil (it helps keep everything from sticking to your skin) and get in there with your bare hands from the very start. Really knead it so everything is coated in a little honey.

Once you're satisfied with the honey to crunchy bits ratio, butter the heck out of a cookie sheet and spread your mix out as thinly as possible. Bake it for about 15 minutes. Use a rubber or silicone spatula to break it all up and mix it around, then try to once more spread it thinly. Pop the mix back in the oven and bake it for another 10-12 minutes, or until it just barely starts to brown. There's a thin line between deliciously crunchy and horrifically burned. When in doubt, undercook the kibble.

While it's still hot, mix in your choice of dried fruit. I'm a big fan of cherries and blueberries, but you're welcome to use cranberries, raisins, pineapple, mango, banana chips, or whatever makes your mouth happy.

Store your homemade kitty kibble in a glass jar or bowl at room temperature for however long you can keep your hands off it. I'm not sure how long it can theoretically last because mine has never survived more than two days.

This is actually a great addition to any Doctor Who themed party. Sprinkle it around whenever you need gravel, a quarry scene, or rocks to set the stage for another food. To serve it on its own, put it in a (clean, new) kitty litter pan and park some Hot Wheels in neat rows along the surface.

Extermination Loaf (S3E5 - Daleks in Manhattan)

1 long French or sourdough baguette
8 tbsp/75 g room temperature butter
½ cup/100 g chocolate chips
½ cup/100 g large edible ball bearings (or mayonnaise)
1 tbsp/15 g cinnamon
4 tbsp/60 g sugar
4 cloves of garlic, minced
1 tsp/5 g salt
chocolate buttons or oversized chocolate chips
white coffee straws
white gumdrops

You can easily make two flavors of this Dalek Bread. If you're taking over Manhattan, enjoy the sweetness of a cinnamon sugar bread with a hint of chocolate on top. If, on the other hand, you're stuck in Hooverville, try some garlic Dalek bread, preferably with slices of genetically modified ham on the side.

Whichever type you want to make, start by cutting your bread about six inches from the end of the loaf. The curved part is your Dalek's head. You'll get two Daleks per baguette (plus a little extra bread to spare.)

Now that you have the bodies, cut four slices, about ⅔ of the way through the bread.

If you're going for the savory version, mix together your minced garlic, salt, and room temperature butter. (You're welcome to add a teaspoon of Herbes de Provence, Italian seasoning, or your favorite garlic bread herb blend.) Generously coat the inside of each slice. According to The Doctor, humans are the only species to invent edible ball bearings. (You can find them in the cake decorating aisle of your grocery store.) In his honor, carefully push them into the bread's crust in order to make the familiar Dalek armor ridges. If you can't find edible ball bearings, you can always resort to dabbing on mayonnaise to symbolize the armor eggs.

If you're making the sweet version, mix your cinnamon, sugar, salt, and butter then generously slather it inside each slice.

Either way, bake your bread for 10 minutes at 400F/205C.

If you're making the sweet version, the moment you pull it from the oven, carefully lay chocolate chips on the surface to make the Dalek armor's dots.

For the finishing touches, start by cutting a white coffee straw in half. Soften a chocolate button or oversized chocolate chip in the microwave (1-2 seconds) then gently press the coffee straw into it. This makes your plunger arm. Poke the arms into your Dalek. If you have pipe cleaners, wrap a scrap of one around one end of the other half of your coffee straw. This makes your eggbeater arm.

Complete the effect by adding a pair of small white gumdrops to the top of the Dalek's head for the antenna. If you have any Cheerios, pretzel sticks, and Nutella at home, you can use those to make an edible eye stalk. Don't stress, though. The antenna and arms are enough to make your Dalek instantly recognizable.

This genuinely edible recipe also happens to be cheap, easy, and darn near guaranteed to illicit a giggle.

Dalek Sec's Head (S6E6 - Evolution of the Daleks)

1 head of cauliflower
8 fat carrots or 8 fat sausages
1 hardboiled egg
1 slice of pitted black olive
3 cups water
1 tsp red food coloring
prepared coleslaw from Series 4, The Doctor's Daughter

This is really more of an edible centerpiece sculpture than a recipe. It's hard to resist making something as oddly grotesque as Dalek Sec's head.

Mix the red food coloring and water. Soak your cauliflower in it overnight, turning it a couple of times to make sure the cauliflower is evenly coated. This will be Dalek Sec's brain. You could always skip this step by substituting a head of red cabbage, but cabbage doesn't quite have the eerily brain-like texture of cauliflower.

The meaty version looks a little more authentic. You'll want to fully cook half a dozen fat sausages. Arrange them around the cauliflower like Dalek Sec's tentacles. Carefully cut the remaining two sausages into strips and arrange them down the middle and across the width of the head, ending in each of the sausages. You may need to carve the sausages a bit in order to make it look like the meaty head strips flow into them naturally. Have fun with it. Worst case scenario, you have to cook a second batch of sausages. Pin everything in place with toothpicks then snip off the ends to maintain the illusion.

If you're a vegetarian or allergic to nitrates, substitute thick peeled carrots for the sausages. If you can find some red carrots at your local farmer's market, you'll still get a lot of the effect, plus you'll impress any of your friends who haven't seen red carrots in real life. (Spoiler alert: they stain anything they're cooked with a dark red, but somehow still taste exactly like ordinary orange carrots.)

Now carefully cut an egg sized hole in your cauliflower or cabbage for Dalek Sec's cyclops eye. Wedge the egg in there nice and tight. Oh so carefully cut another hole in your hardboiled egg for the olive pupil. You can also substitute a googly eye from the cake decorating section of your grocery store.

The first time I made this, I tried to get clever by putting the cauliflower on top of an extra wide can wrapped in nori (seaweed paper used to wrap sushi.) That way, the sausages would hang down, looking even more tentacle-like. It was a great theory, but in reality, I couldn't get the sausages to stay in place, no matter how many strategically placed (and artfully cut) toothpicks I tried to use to nail them down.

Instead, I'm content to simply arrange the top of his head on a bed of coleslaw, surrounded by bread Daleks. Remember the middle parts of the baguette you used to make your bread Daleks? They can be pressed into service here. Simply toast them up and spread a little horseradish on the inside. When people are ready to eat, they can stuff one of Dalek Sec's sausage tentacles into the impromptu bun, top it with the coleslaw beneath his head, and enjoy a somewhat cannibalistic sandwich.

Lazarus Cocktail (S3E7 - The Lazarus Experiment)

2 shots/90 ml blueberry vodka
2 shots/90 ml tonic water
yellow sugar
fresh blueberries
ice

Drink this and you'll either feel young again or turn into a social monster. You won't know which until you try it. To make this simple, attractive cocktail, start by quickly dipping a lowball glass in water and putting it in the freezer. The goal here is to get a nice frosted glass full of bluish fluid, much like the Youth-O-Tron Dr. Lazarus emerged from. It just so happens that the colors also work nicely with the Tardis colors, giving this cocktail an even more Whovian flair.

If your grocery store doesn't stock dyed sugar in the baking aisle, it's easy to make your own. Just mix 4-6 drops (depending on how hard you squeeze) of yellow food coloring into 1/4 cup of sugar. Use a fork to mix it heartily until the dye is evenly distributed over all the granules. You can use it for all kinds of decorating - or you can go crazy and make a heck of a lot of cocktails for your friends. Once you have a frosty glass and a pile of sparkly yellow sugar, get two tea saucers or salad plates. Fill one with water and the other with your yellow sugar. Dip your frosted glass in the water then dip it into the yellow sugar. Congrats! You now have a frosted glass with a yellow sugar rim. All you need now is a drink to fill it.

Carefully pour in the blueberry vodka. If you can't find blueberry vodka, take a hammer to a bag of frozen blueberries so they get nice and crushed, let the bag come to room temperature, and strain out the blueberry juice. This may seem complicated, but I can't find affordable blueberry juice in any local grocery while I can find oodles of frozen blueberries for around $3 per bag. You can substitute one shot of the blueberry juice and one shot of vodka for the blueberry vodka, all the while pretending that you're the sort of person who only uses whole, organic, natural ingredients to make a cocktail.

Now add a scant handful of unhammered frozen blueberries (or fresh, if you're using premade blueberry vodka) to the bottom of the glass. Add your nice, bubbly tonic tonic water. Gently stir the cocktail so everything is mixed. Be careful not to knock off the sugar resting on the rim. Top it off with a few cubes of ice. Drink a couple of these and you'll feel younger, smarter, and more attractive ... right up until the point where you turn into a giant humanoid insect.

Burnt Custard Sun (S3E8 - 42)

4 egg yolks
1/2 cup/65 g sugar + 6 tsp/30 g sugar for the topping
3 tsp/15 ml vanilla extract
2 cups/480 ml heavy whipping cream

"Burn with me," as you fall into the sun. In the United States, this dessert would be called Creme Brulee, but in the spirit of the episode, we're using the British Name: Burnt Custard. The smooth flesh will melt in your mouth just like the crew of the S.S. *Pentallian* as they fall into the star they illegally mined.

The good news is burnt custard is a lot easier than most people think. In a small saucepan, warm the cream over a medium heat until bubbles start to form around the edges. The goal here isn't to boil the milk. You want to keep it nice and smooth. While the cream is gently heating, whisk your egg yolks and sugar together in a bowl. Once the cream starts to bubble at the edges, pull the pan off the heat and stir in the egg yolk mixture. Gently mix it together. Add in the vanilla, then keep mixing it some more.

Heavily butter half a dozen small ramekins. Equally distribute the custard between the ramekins. Place the ramekins in a baking pan, and add one inch of boiling water. Put the pan in an oven and bake the custards at 350F/177C for 40-45 minutes, or until the center is set enough that the middle barely jiggles. Take the ramekins out of the pan and let them rest for 10 minutes. Cover them with foil, then put them in a fridge for at least 4 hours, or overnight. Before serving, sprinkle the top of each burnt custard with one teaspoon of sugar. Pop them under a hot broiler and let them cook for two to five minutes, or until the sugar is caramelized and browned, but not burnt. If you have a kitchen torch, have fun using that to caramelize the sugar instead. Any excuse to cook with fire is a good one.

Scarecrow Soldiers (S3E9 - Human Nature)

Popcorn Balls:
18 cups/150 g popped popcorn
2 cups/450 g sugar
1 1/3 cups/310 ml water
½ cup/170 ml light corn syrup
1 tsp/5 ml white vinegar
1 tsp/5 ml vanilla
½ tsp/2.5 g salt

Scarecrow Coating:
2 cups/900 g creamy peanut butter
shredded wheat cereal or corn flakes
regular sized chocolate chips
mini chocolate chips

Close to Halloween, Americans can find pre-made popcorn balls alongside the rest of the seasonal bagged candy. Feel free to save yourself some hassle by purchasing them. The rest of the year, you're going to have to make these for yourself, just like Whovians all over the rest of the world. Luckily, it's not that hard.

Fill all your largest bowls about halfway with popped popcorn. It's okay if you look like half your kitchen is spread out on your dining room table.

Once that's done, pour your corn syrup, water, vinegar and sugar into a saucepan. Cook it all over a high heat until it reaches 255F/124C on a candy thermometer or achieves the "hard ball" state of candy making. If the Tardis matrix won't translate that into real cooking terms for you, just stir frequently until the sugar is completely dissolved and everything seems pretty thick. The recipe is forgiving. Just before you take the mix off the heat, stir in the vanilla.

Now quickly and carefully pour the sugary mix over your popcorn. Try to drizzle it as evenly as possible over as much of the popcorn as you can. This is why you're using so many bowls. Toss each bowl gently so the popcorn within is evenly coated. Once you're out of syrup and all your popcorn has been tossed, it's time to turn it into ovals. You were expecting balls, but honestly, the scarecrows in this episode had decidedly squarish rounded heads.

As soon as the mix is cool enough to touch, grease your hands up with butter or olive oil (for the vegans and vegetarians). Press the popcorn into baseball sized balls. Squeeze the balls into more rounded off rectangles or ovals. Just make sure the bottom is flat so they'll stay upright when served. These will become your scarecrow heads. Let them cool on a sheet of waxed paper.

Go wash your hands and get your scarecrow coating ready. This part is pretty easy, too.

Soften your two cups of peanut butter in the microwave. You don't want to cook it. The goal here is to temporarily turn it into a thick liquid. Stir and check it every 15-30 seconds. While your peanut butter is softening, crumble two cups of your shredded wheat or corn flakes. This will provide the straw texture for your scarecrow heads.

Now roll each popcorn ball in the peanut butter. Put the peanut buttery balls on a sheet of waxed paper. While the peanut butter is still plenty soft, arrange the crumbled cereal along the base so it looks like straw sticking out of stuffed shirt collar. You can also add a knot of butcher's twine so it looks like you've tied a sack closed around the scarecrow heads. Use the full sized chocolate chips for eyes and the mini chocolate chips to make a mouth.

If you'd like, feel free to substitute Rice Krispie treats for the popcorn balls. I found them too sweet, even though the shapes worked better. Regardless of their interior, these deceptively cute sugar soldiers will break both your hearts.

Family of Blood(y Mary) (S3E10 - The Family of Blood)

1.5 shots/70 ml vodka
3 shots/135 ml tomato juice
1 tbsp/15 ml fresh lemon juice
1 tsp/5 ml dill pickle juice
½ tsp/2.5 g prepared horseradish
¼ tsp/1 g celery salt
¼ tsp/1 g fresh ground black pepper
healthy dash Worcestershire sauce (6-7 shakes)
3 drops hot sauce
pinch salt
celery stick
carrot
beef jerky

If you've just had 900 years of memories shockingly restored so you can save England from body stealing monsters, this is just the drink you need to take the edge off. In the spirit of authenticity, I could've offered you the same tea Martha offered Jenny, but somehow, adding a little mutton and a nice bit of gravy to the pot didn't appeal to me - especially not after she offered to top it off with sardines and jam.

Instead, dump everything but the celery stick, carrot, and beef jerky in a tall glass. Give it a healthy stir, then top the glass off with ice. The Doctor would naturally need some celery in his Bloody Mary, but you can also add half a salad in there if you want. Carrots, cheese cubes on a stick, and beef jerky make this into a surprisingly healthy drinkable sandwich with a mellow kick.

If you're not in the mood to make it yourself, threaten some bright, younger students at your boarding school until they mix one up for you. This fortifying drink will nourish your body while helping your mind cope with the most improbable madness your village has ever witnessed.

Weeping Angel Wings (S3E11 - Blink)

20 chicken wings
¾ cup/100 g flour
½ cup/114 g melted butter
½ cup/110 ml hot sauce of your choice
1 tsp/ 5 g salt
½ tsp/2.5 g cayenne pepper
4 cloves of garlic, minced

Let's be honest. You're not going to make hot wings from scratch. The time and hassle aren't worth it. You're going to pick up a bucket of them from KFC or have a box of them delivered from Pizza Hut. If you're feeling really fancy, you might even pick up some wild flavored ones from your favorite sports bar.

I know this. You know this. But since this is a cookbook, we're going to make a pact right now. Let's pretend you wanted a moderately healthy version of Weeping Angel Wings instead of the usual deep fried buffalo wings. Out of respect for your guest's arteries, you went to the immense hassle and extra expense of making these yourself. Gosh, you're amazing. I'm really impressed.

While we're playing make believe, let's pretend you put your flour, cayenne pepper, and salt in a ginormous resealable plastic bag. Blow some extra air in the bag, seal it tight, and shake it madly until everything is well mixed.

Next, line a baking sheet with aluminum foil then coat that with some butter or oil. Remember, I said this was a moderately healthy version. If you don't coat your aluminum foil, these things will stick and you'll be stuck eating metal.

Now set up a nice little assembly line. You have your chicken wings, a bowl of water, your bag of lightly seasoned flour, and your buttered cookie sheet. Dunk 2-3 of the wings in water, throw them in your plastic bag, seal it tight, and shake it about. Carefully pull out your wings and arrange them in a neat, single layer on your cookie sheet. This way, you get flour into every nook and crevice of the wing.

Once all your chicken is coated, put the baking sheet in your refrigerator for at least an hour. This is a good time to once more ask yourself why you're not just buying some of these. Oh, right. You're a culinary perfectionist who loves healthy cooking. Remember that when you're cleaning hot sauce out from under your fingernails.

After an hour (or up to 6 if you have a life), preheat your oven to 400F/150C. While that's warming up it's time to mix your hot sauce, garlic, and melted butter. Give it a good, solid beating, the sort you probably feel you deserve for going to all this unnecessary hassle.

Once you're satisfied, pull the baking sheet of wings back out of the fridge. Carefully dunk each one into the butter and hot sauce mix. Try to coat as much of it as possible, but don't go nuts. You don't want to lose the flour coating. That's what gives it a fake crispiness. Put each wing back on the cookie sheet after its hot sauce bath.

Once all the wings are coated, bake them for 25 minutes. Flip each one over then put them back in the oven and bake them for another 25 minutes. Serve them on a platter decorated with grey colored cake batter to resemble ground and chipped gravel. Or, being realistic, just wrap some blue paper around your KFC bucket. Either way, garnish your wings with a pair of mirrored sunglasses. After all, you don't have to worry about blinking when the angel you're stalking is staring at itself.

Professor Yana's Gluten Neutrino Map Binder (S3E12 - Utopia)

1 package dark whole wheat fettuccine
¼ cup/60 ml olive oil
1 tbsp/30 g basil pesto
2 garlic cloves, minced
1 tsp/5 g salt
fried crickets, optional

Maybe I'm just a sucker for Derek Jacobi, but I found myself feeling incredibly sorry for The Master in this episode. He's had a whole, long human life full of scientific achievements and philanthropy. One glance into his Gallifreyan watch, and suddenly none of that mattered anymore. One minute, he's crazy brilliant. The next, he's just crazy. C'mon, the guy is so smart he made a computer out of pasta.

So can you.

This recipe won't turn you into a genocidal maniac unless you're irrationally enraged by fiber. Find the darkest, densest whole wheat pasta in your grocery store. (If you hate fiber but love presentation, you can substitute some black squid ink fettuccine.)

I mixed buckwheat and whole wheat to get some color contrast. Whatever you pick, boil it according to the package directions.

While the pasta boils, mix your olive oil, basil pesto, salt, and freshly minced garlic in a large bowl. Once you've cooked, drained, and rinsed the pasta, dump it into the olive oil mix and stir it about until the noodles are all well coated.

For presentation, set a roasting rack on its side and drape individual noodles over it to create the Gluten Neutrino Map Binder. I used a leftover cheese wedge to help keep my roasting rack from getting too wobbly. You're welcome to try aluminum foil or, if you aren't trying to keep the dish vegetarian, some kind of meat.

Pool the rest of the noodles in the bottom of the pan and drizzle any leftover olive oil sauce on top. Coating pasta in olive oil is one of the best ways to keep it moist and edible at room temperature, so don't worry about your pasta drying out into mysterious and inedible stalks.

If you're so inclined, honor the poor, fallen Chantho by serving this with a side of fried crickets. You probably can't use it to navigate a spaceship from the end of the universe, but put on a steampunky vest and enjoy a couple cocktails and you can certainly fake it.

Cucumber Drums of Madness (S3E13 - The Sound of Drums)

2 long, straight cucumbers
1 8 oz/220 g package of cream cheese
2 tbsp/30 g mixed herbs of your choice

In honor of The Master's return to madness, serve your guests these easy miniature drums. They'll knock four times against the walls of your arteries, but the creamy flavor is worth it.

Cut the rounded ends off your cucumbers. Now, carefully peel some lines in the cucumbers so the exterior looks like a green drum with white strut supports. Cut it into neat, two inch slices then hollow out the middle of each one. I like to use a melon baller so I can leave a little bit of cucumber at the bottom to hold in the filling. Cut some spare slices of cucumber for the top of the drums.

Mix ¾ of your cream cheese with your herbs. If that's too much hassle, just pick up your favorite white spreadable cheese from the grocery store (Boursin, for example, is easy to use and comes in a lot of good flavors.)

Fill your drum most of the way, then cap it off with some plain cream cheese so the top stays nice and white. Use a butter knife to spread the nice white cheese as flat as possible. Top it with a round slice of cucumber. For an added touch, arrange two toothpicks on top as drum sticks.

Cantaloupe Toclafane (S3E14 - The Last of the Time Lords)

2 cantaloupes
1 pear
blueberries
assorted blue, red, and clear wires or drinking straws
aluminum foil

In the spirit of authenticity, I should've given you a recipe for the cold, mashed swede The Master feeds Jack Harkness, or at least the fish and chips he asks for instead. However, I really didn't want to waste hours in my kitchen experimenting with cold, mashed swede recipes that I knew no one would make. Instead, you're getting another sculpture project.

Now, if you happen to have a classic brass birdcage and a large doll dressed in a suit, you have a good 900 year old shriveled Doctor decoration. Pop off the head and substitute a small cantaloupe instead. You can pose the doll inside the birdcage so it looks like it's gripping the wrinkly cantaloupe head in agony.

Most of us don't have old fashioned bird cages and creepy dolls lying about the house, though, so you can substitute this incredibly edible Toclafane head sculpture.

Cut one cantaloupe in half and scoop out all the guts. This one will be the shell of your Toclafane sphere.

Cut the second cantaloupe in half. Scoop out the guts then carefully peel off the skin. You should have some nice orange flesh.

Use two wide wedges to make the cheeks. Use your aluminum foil to make a tapered triangular breathing mask between them. Now cut two smaller wedges to make the cheekbones. You'll position those on top of the cheeks.

Next peel your pear. The white flesh makes the Toclafane's eyes. Cut almond shaped eye pieces and position them above the crescent shaped cantaloupe cheekbones. You don't want the eyes to be too sunken. If they're not high enough up, pad the bottom with some extra cantaloupe meat.

Now take the remaining half of your second cucumber. It should be a nice roughly peeled half sphere of orange flesh. Cut away what you need in order to fit it into the gutted cucumber shell. You want it to be flush with the pear eye slices while also completely filling the shell.

Use your extra pieces of cucumber to flesh out the face and wedge it in nicely. Once it's fully formed, use the tines of a fork to carve deep forehead lines. Use a butter knife or one tine of the fork to carve a long oval, about two inches wide, into the middle of the forehead. Go ahead and add any more wrinkles or lines you'd like.

Finish it off by mashing two blueberries flat and carefully pressing them into the middle of the eyes as dark, cloudy pupils.

If you're careful, you should be able to get two Toclafane from two cantaloupes. If you're not - and I'll be honest, this is a bit of a hassle the first time around - you'll get one Toclafane and a bunch of cantaloupe chunks. That's fine. Serve your one Toclafane surrounded by a mix of cantaloupe chunks and blueberries. If people ask, they're there to symbolize the fiery skies filled with dead stars that wait at the end of the universe, but you and I know there're really there to give your guests something to nosh on so your Toclafane has a chance of surviving until the last stragglers wander in. After all, something like this is worth showing off.

SERIES FOUR: THE DOCTOR-DONNA

Titanic 1st Class Menu Punch Romaine (S4E1 - Voyage of the Damned)

6 cups/2.7 kilograms crushed ice
2 cups/475 ml Champagne or sparkling wine
1 cup/237 ml white wine
1 cup/237 ml simple syrup
1/3 cup/78 ml fresh orange juice
2 tbsp/30 ml lemon juice
2 tbsp/30 ml white rum
orange peel (optional)

There was so much food in this episode I had a hard time deciding what to make. Foon's Buffalo Wings were tempting, but I've already given you a recipe for Weeping Angel Wings. If Rambutan Fruit was easily available it'd be perfect as a stand in for Banacafalata. In the end, since this episode takes place on the sinking Titanic, it seemed appropriate to give you an easy recipe you can make at home for something first class passengers on board the real Titanic would've considered schmancy.

Once upon a time, this proto-margarita would've been an expensive and time consuming drink. Luckily, you have a blender. Modern technology is wonderful. You can skip all that thankless labor and simply toss everything but the orange peel into the blender. Leave the ingredients at the tender mercy of your whirring steel blades for about a minute. Once you have a nicely alcoholic ice mix, spoon it into individual dessert cups.

You're on a boat. That means unless you're wearing a captain's hat, you're not the designated driver. Enjoy the luxury of knowing you won't be behind the wheel tonight by drizzling another half a shot of rum over the ice cups. To keep it classy, garnish each one with a curl of orange peel.

If you'd rather have a less classy but more evocative garnish, you can serve these with some easy Host Haloes. Toast up some white bread until its golden brown. Use a large glass to cut halo sized circles and a small glass to cut out the interior. Smear the circle of toast with clear apple jelly for that shiny golden look. Garnish each glass with a halo. Whenever someone asks you for information, remind them they're about to die.

Serve these quickly lest you risk the dessert melting and the Host decapitating you in the hallway.

Adipose Herbed Butter (S4E2 - Partners in Crime)

1/2 cup/114 g undyed butter
2 tbsp/30 g Herbs de Provence
2 tbsp/30 ml fresh lemon juice
2 tsp/10 g pepper
½ tsp/2.5 g salt
small blueberries

Oh, Adipose. Your squishy adorableness has so much potential. Adipose Rice Crispy treats were tempting, but they weren't smooth enough. A bento box filled with cuddly Adipose shaped sushi rice came out adorable and tasty, but still had a little more texture than I liked.

If you really want the smooth, creamy texture of the Adipose, you need to be true to the monsters. You need to work with pure, delicious fat.

Butter isn't naturally yellow. That's just dye. Most fresh butter is actually a creamy white color. Pick up some fresh butter from a farmer's market or, if your local grocery stocks undyed butter, pick up some of that. Regardless of where you get it, when you bring your butter home, let it sit at room temperature. You want it soft, but not melted.

Knead the salt, Herbes de Provence, and lemon juice into half of the butter. At this point, it should look way too herby to pass for an Adipose. Luckily, you have the other half pound of butter.

Shape your herb butter into a rough oval. Now carefully mash your remaining butter around it until you have a deceptively smooth white outer shell. Cut a slit on each side to make the arms and a slit down the middle bottom to make the legs. Pack them with more fresh butter until you don't have any herbs showing. You're basically sculpting a rounded fatty square with limbs.

Once your Adipose butter sculpture is the right shape, it's time for the details. Carefully use your thumbs to create a crease for the eyes. You can use a thumbnail to make a thin line for the mouth. Fill the mouth with a dense line of black pepper.

Now for the hard part. Get a cheap paint brush and carefully paint on the black pepper powder to shadow the eyes. Trust me, this makes a huge difference in the overall appearance of the Adipose. Once your eyes are shadowed, carefully push a small blueberry in place for the pupil.

Now, if you're going for extreme accuracy, you'll want to give your Adipose a faint pink hue around the edges. If your local grocery stocks powdered sumac at affordable prices, pick up a bottle of that and a second cheap, disposable paintbrush. Sumac is a reddish Persian spice that just so happens to create a wonderful fleshy blush color when used in very modest quantities. Go gently with it. You just want to add some highlights. If your local grocery doesn't stock sumac, don't panic. Your Adipose will still be an instantly recognizable buttery delight. You can also use paprika or chili powder, but those flavors tend to overwhelm the herbs.

Once you're finished, loosely tent some waxed paper over your Adipose and put it back in the fridge to stiffen up until right before your party.

Now, if you don't happen to like Herbes de Provence, you can substitute whatever seasonings you want in the middle of your Adipose. Just make sure you use a little bit more than seems sensible so the unseasoned outer shell won't dilute the flavor too badly. I'm a big fan of freshly minced garlic with some onion flakes, generic "Italian" seasoning mix, dill and chives, or rosemary and basil. Really, whatever spices you normally cook with will work fine when making your own seasoned butter.

Marble Circuits With Fire Dipping Sauce (S4E3 - The Fires of Pompeii)

1 14 oz/400 g can of chickpeas/garbanzo beans, drained
½ cup/120 g roasted red bell peppers, drained
⅓ cup/80 g tahini
⅓ cup/80 ml lemon juice
2 tbsp/30 ml olive oil
2 cloves of garlic, peeled
½ tsp/2.5 g salt
smooth surfaced cucumbers

It seems like 90% of ancient Roman recipes were based on a nine year old boy's dare. Rather than make you gag through a recipe for authentic garam fish sauce, I thought you'd prefer something inexpensive to make, easier to eat, and instantly recognizable to your dedicated Whovians..

The small circuits are surprisingly easy to make. You need some smooth skinned American style cucumbers Look for the widest ones you can find, preferably more oval than round

Slice your cucumber in half length wise. Use a spoon to hollow out the seeds. What you have left is the right color for the marble circuits (green on top, white beneath) but entirely the wrong shape. You want to carve the white interior flesh until you have leveled things out so your cucumber slice is as flat as possible.

Once you have a flat-ish rectangle, use the tines of a very solid fork to carve lines into the skin. The easiest thing to do is just carve a couple of circular holes in each corner, make a short diagonal line going inwards, angle it sharply downwards, then fill in all the extra spaces with straight lines. Have fun playing with it. If you do this continuously along the width of the cucumber, you can then cut the rectangle down into interlocking squares. Depending on the size and shape of your cucumber, you should be able to get at least 12 circuits.

Once you get the hang of it, carving the cucumbers goes faster than you think. It's best to go ahead and carve up at least 4 cucumbers at a time then encourage your guests to try and make an entire computer motherboard out of them.

With all that carving work to look forward to, you and I both know you're just going to pick up a tub of roasted red pepper hummus at the grocery store. Maybe, if you're feeling extra fancy, you'll grab some nice bloody looking roasted red bell peppers to go with it. However, this is a cookbook, so let's pretend you're going to make your own hummus.

Luckily for you, hummus is almost comically simple. Just throw everything but the cucumbers into a blender or food processor and let the machine attack the food with its angry blades until you have a nice, smooth paste.

Since you'll have extra roasted red bell peppers left over from making your hummus (wink), serve your cucumber circuits surrounded by the hot red lava colored vegetables on one side and the cooling lava colored red bell pepper hummus on the other.

The Sibylline priestesses predict your guests will polish off this appetizer.

Ood Mezze Plate (S4E4 - Planet of the Ood)

1 jar roasted red bell pepper strips
2 packages hummus
2 hard boiled eggs
1 long piece of string cheese
1 package pita
raisins

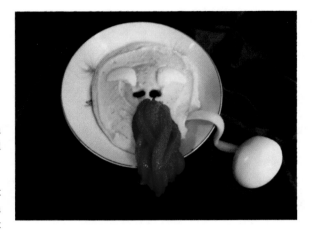

While you're playing with your food by making stone circuits, you might as well set up another highly recognizable appetizer tray inspired by the tentacle-tastic Ood.

This is a great one to throw together fast and cheap if, say, you thought only 5 people were coming to your viewing party but for some reason you discovered 20 unexpected RSVP's this morning. It's a super fast sculpting project good for people with kludgy hands. Honestly, the hardest part is boiling the eggs.

Grab your largest plate. Now scoop out all the hummus and make a rough oval in the middle. This works best if your hummus is kind of pinkish (roasted red pepper, for example) or a darker grey-brown (olive tapenade, herb infused, etc.) Plain hummus won't offer enough color contrast with the pita.

Now cut one of your eggs in half. You now have two Ood eyes. Plop them in the pool of hummus. If you want, you can try to carefully dot the back of a couple olive rounds with hummus (which will act as a sort of food glue) and put them on the eggs as pupils. Add a couple of raisins for the nostrils.

To make the mouth, empty the oil out of the roasted red bell peppers and rinse them all off thoroughly. Your hands will still be kind of greasy, so be careful when handling a knife. You want to cut the peppers into thin, tentacle-like strips. Once you have a nice mound of strips, arrange them so they're spilling out of your Ood's mouth.

Cut your pita loaves into wedges and arrange them neatly along the sides of your plate, basically filling up any space that isn't taken up by the Ood's face.

Finally, stretch a piece of white string cheese until it reaches from the Ood's mouth to an adjacent tea saucer. Cut a small slit into the egg and stuff one end of the string cheese inside. If you're a particularly benevolent Ood master, instead of the artificial brain sphere you can alternately arrange salmon slices or Spam in the shape of a wet pink brain.

If you're feeling extra fancy, you could always boil up a dozen eggs, buy a couple jars of roasted red bell pepper strips, and have a salad plate (or tea saucer) sized personal Ood servant waiting for each of your guests at a sit down dinner. It's honestly not much more hassle than the single big Ood platter. You just need more tasty external brains.

Sontaran Soldiers (S4E5 - The Sontaran Stratagem)

6 russet baking potatoes (jacket potatoes for UK readers)
6 tbsp/180 g butter
12 tbsp/180 g kosher salt or coarse sea salt
12 blue cupcake tins
12 almonds
small frozen blueberries
ketchup

Additions:
½ cup or equally sized small serving bowls of toppings such as:
butter
chives
sour cream
bacon bits
shredded cheese

Admit it. The first time you saw the Sontarans, you found yourself craving a fresh baked potato. Luckily for you, that means you have a super simple, easily recognizable, totally Whovian recipe that doesn't require any special ingredients. As a bonus, it's even made of things people will actually eat. If any of your guests don't instantly recognize these guys, they're lying about their love of Doctor Who.

There are two ways to make baked potatoes; the fast way and the delicious way. The fast way is to simply poke the potato with a fork a few times and microwave it into oblivion. You can do that if you're really crunched for time, but for the purposes of this recipe, I'm going to pretend you opted for the delicious way instead.

Preheat your oven to 400F. While it's heating, give your potatoes a good, firm scrubbing. You want to get rid of any residual dirt and, as it happens, texturize the skins slightly at the same time.

Once all your potatoes are nice and clean, rub each one down with a tablespoon of butter. It's okay if you have some butter left over as long as you've thoroughly coated the potatoes. Now that they're nice and buttery, rub each potato down with two tablespoons of coarse kosher or sea salt.

Arrange your potatoes on a foil lined baking sheet. Bake them at 400F/205C for one hour.

While your potatoes are merrily baking away, fill half a dozen small serving bowls with your choice of baked potato toppings; butter, bacon bits, chives, sour cream, salsa, cheese, diced onions, or whatever you like on a potato.

When the baked potatoes are finished, take them out of the oven and let them rest for at least 10 minutes. Brush off the excess salt, cut each potato in half, and put the halves cut side down into a blue cupcake tin. If you're really lucky, your grocery might even have the blue metallic cupcake tins, which add a really nice touch. Either way, your potato in its blue collar already looks like a Sontaran. Complete the effect by adding a couple finishing details.

First, push the almond into the upper middle of the face for the nose. Next, cut two horizontal slits just above the nose. Push your frozen blueberries in place for the eyes. Don't use fresh blueberries. You want something that can stand up to some pressure. To make the mouth, carve a squared frown just below the nose. Pull the skin out slightly and add a little catsup to really define the mouth.

You now have a dozen Sontaran soldiers to serve your guests, should they be worthy. All hail Sontar!

Clone Vat Cocktail (S4E6 - The Poison Sky)

1 shot mango rum
1 shot coconut rum
2 bananas
1 cup fresh spinach
½ cup coconut milk
½ cup frozen peaches
½ cup ice
½ tsp/2.5 g cinnamon

You don't have to be a force grown Sontaran clone to enjoy this cocktail. It has your birth vat's same thick, creamy texture and clearly alien greenness alongside some mind altering rum to help you forget whether you're the original or the clone.

This is even easier than growing a spare Martha Jones. Set aside one banana. Throw everything else into a blender. I promise you won't be able to taste the spinach. It's there for color, and it works beautifully. Plus, between the banana, spinach, and peaches, you can honestly say you've had your daily servings of fruits and vegetables in one glass. If you want to celebrate by tossing in a third shot of pineapple rum, I think you well deserve it.

While the blender turns your solids into liquids, slice your banana in half lengthwise. Put the long banana garnishes into two glasses, fill them up with the Clone Vat Cocktail, and find someone to share with. If you're feeling extra fancy you can add a small nugget of dry ice so the cocktail will smoke like an Atmos equipped car.

Baked Hath Served over Black Beans & Topped with a Red and Green Cabbage Slaw. (S4E7 - The Doctor's Daughter)

Fish:
2 tilapia filets
4 tbsp/60 ml orange juice
1 tbsp/15 ml olive oil
4 cloves of garlic, minced
1 tsp/5 g salt
½ tsp/2.5 g red pepper flakes

Slaw:
1/4 head of red cabbage
1/3 head of green cabbage
2 tbsp/30 ml rice wine vinegar
2 tbsp/30 ml orange juice
1 tbsp/15 ml sesame oil
1 tbsp/15 g mayonnaise
1 tbsp/15 g sugar
1 tsp/5 g ginger powder
½ tsp/2.5 g salt

Black Beans:
1 14 oz/400 g can of black beans
½ cup/220 g cooked yellow corn/maize
1 tomato, diced
½ onion, diced
2 cloves garlic, minced
1 tsp/5 g cumin
Juice of ½ lime

I humbly present a dish inspired by the alien who saved Martha Jones from drowning in quicksand. The fish is for the Hath, the black beans for the sludge he drowned in, and the red and green cabbage slaw for the colors of the Hath's scales.

Now, there are two ways to make this dish; the tasty way and the fast way. For the fast way, just buy yourself some frozen tilapia in mango sauce, grab a can of black beans, and pick up a tub of coleslaw at the deli counter. Let's make it the tasty way instead.

For the fish, whisk together everything but the tilapia in a shallow bowl. Once you have a bowl of tasty citrus goodness, coat both sides of the fish as thoroughly as possible, then leave it soaking in the marinade for at least an hour.

While the fish is soaking, make the coleslaw. If you've never made coleslaw from scratch, I promise it's a lot easier than you think. For this one, mix everything but the cabbage in a large bowl. Blend it all as thoroughly as possible. While those ingredients are cheerfully mingling, it's time to take a hatchet to the cabbages. If you have a large chef's knife or, if you're very lucky, a butcher knife, making coleslaw is fun. You can roughly dice it into squares, precisely cut it into nice, long slivers, or you can go crazy just hacking away at it in a mad frenzy of vegetative destruction until you come out of your fugue state and find a pile of thin cabbagy slices in front of you. I won't judge.

Mix the two types of cabbage together then throw them in the bowl with your dressing and do your best to coat all the cabbage. This isn't a thick, gloppy dressing. It should be light, even a little thin, creating an aromatic coating. Let the coleslaw sit at room temperature until the fish is fully cooked so the flavors will have plenty of time to mingle.

Finally, make the black beans. Watching Martha's poor Hath friend drown in that lumpy, black sludge inspired this recipe to begin with. Mix everything but the beans into a bowl. Stir it hard, until everything is well blended. Drain the can of black beans then add them to the bowl and gently coat them with the mix. It's pretty easy. By now, your fish should be nicely marinated. Preheat an oven to 400F/205C. Coat the bottom of a glass baking dish with butter or olive oil. Put the fish in the dish, pour the marinade on top, and bake it uncovered for 20 minutes or until the fish flakes easily with a fork.

This makes two hearty servings. Divide the black beans between two plates and spread them into a neat oval. Top the black beans with your freshly baked fish. If there's any sauce at the bottom of the pan, spoon a tablespoon or two onto each tilapia filet. Top the tilapia with a carefully arranged handful of the fresh slaw and fill in the rest of the plate with extra slaw.

You now have the entire episode capsulated on one plate. To complete the effect, this dish is best served with a lime green Jell-O shot.

Timelord Cyanide Detox Platter (S4E8 - The Unicorn and the Wasp)

ginger beer
anchovies
walnuts
salted almonds
olives
pickles
salty ham or thin sliced prosciutto
smoked salmon slices

If you ever need to stimulate inhibited enzymes into reversal because you've been poisoned with cyanide, don't try to heal yourself with a Harvey Wallbanger. Also, don't take medical advice from a show about aliens. If you happen to be a Time Lord, what you probably need is a big shock, but first, you'll want to stuff yourself with protein and salt.

This makes an easy appetizer platter for hardcore Whovians. The Doctor guzzled a bottle of ginger beer before chowing down on anchovies for salt and walnuts for protein. Once you've arranged those on a plate, you can add whatever salty, high protein foods you want. Since this episode was set in the roaring twenties, other period finger foods would've included salted almonds, olives, pickles, smoked salmon, and thin sliced prosciutto or ham. If that's a little too much salt and protein for you, nearly every food related scene in this episode featured a fruit bowl with green and purple grapes, red apples, and some oranges for extra color.

This appetizer platter is best served with a sidecar in honor of Donna Noble or The Doctor's preferred lime soda if you're driving the Tardis home tonight. If you're worried about vespiforms invading your party, sneak a little fresh ground pepper into the platter.

Vashta Nerada Detection Kit (S4E9 - Silence in the Library)

bag of mixed green salad
dressing of your choice
8 chicken legs/drumsticks
2 tbsp/30 ml Worcestershire sauce
1 tbsp/15 g prepared dijon mustard
1 tbsp/15 ml olive oil
1 tsp/5 g black pepper
4 garlic cloves, minced

Consider this highly portable meal your security blanket against the darkness. If you're afraid of something in the shadows, toss one of the drumsticks into the dark. If you end up with hair on your food, you're safe. If the shadows clean the meat off the bones, get a flashlight because you're in danger from the Vashta Nerada.

Most dollar stores stock plain metal boxes with lids. You can just as easily substitute any disposable rectangular plastic-ware dishes. The great thing about this dish is it's a super cheap, super easy, super recognizable way to serve all your guests a main course they'll instantly recognize.

Now, you and I both know you're going to pick up a box of spring mix at the grocery store along with a few pre-cooked drumsticks. I personally think that if you throw in a Slitheen egg and a couple of marble circuit board cucumbers, you have a nutritious and fetching bento-box worth taking to work or school.

On the off chance you want to cook this from scratch but have never baked chicken drumsticks before, you're in for a surprisingly cheap and easy main course. Chicken legs tend to be one of the cheapest cuts available in most grocery stores, yet ironically the most forgiving to new cooks.

Preheat your oven to 450F/233C. While your oven warms up, mix your Worcestershire, mustard, pepper, olive oil, and garlic in a large bowl. Give it a good, thorough whisking so the flavors play nicely together.

Now cover a baking sheet with aluminum foil and either butter it up or hose it down with nonstick spray. Roll each of your chicken legs in the sauce mix, taking care to get them as nicely coated as possible. If you're lazy or busy, you can always do your best to coat all the chicken legs then leave them in the fridge to marinate for anywhere from a few hours to overnight. If you're in a hurry, just coat them and pop them in the oven.

Let the chicken legs bake for about 25 minutes, or until the juices run clear when poked with a sharp knife. If there's any evidence of pink in the juices, put your chicken legs back in the oven for another 5 minutes.

Once they're baked, you can serve them either hot or cold. For presentation sake, I can vouch that putting these on a bed of lightly dressed salad greens and serving them in a metal box will leave your guests staring suspiciously at the shadows all night long.

River Song (S4E10 - Forest of the Dead)

6 hardboiled eggs
6 angel hair pasta nests
6 tbsp/180 g butter
6 garlic cloves, minced
2 tsp/10 g kosher salt or coarse sea salt
juice of 1 lemon
roasted red bell peppers
olives

I freaking love this dish. Making it is simplicity itself. Whovians crack up when they see it. Plus, as an extra bonus, it makes a good main course for octo-lavo vegetarians (people who eat eggs and butter but not meat.)

First, hardboil your eggs. This isn't terribly exciting. Add half a dozen eggs to a pan of cold water (if any of them float they've gone bad. You'll want to throw them away and get new eggs). Bring the water to a boil. As soon as it boils, promptly turn off the heat, put a lid on the pan, and leave it alone for the next 10 minutes. After that, just drain the eggs, refill your pot with cold water, and leave them to cool while you work on the rest of the recipe.

If you can find angel hair pasta nests, they make this dish so easy. If you can't, seriously don't panic. Just pick up a regular box of angel hair pasta and prepare to get a little personal when twining it into shape. If you can find the nests, the tricky part is making sure you use a gentle hand. Boil the angel hair pasta nests according to the package directions. When the package says not to stir the angel hair nests too heavily, believe it. You want to have nice, neat nests when you're done, not carefully detangled strands of noodles. Just drop the nests into boiling water, maybe push them under a couple times if they bob to the surface, and otherwise leave them alone while they boil.

Once the pasta nests are finished, carefully lift them from the water with a slotted spoon. Leave them on a plate to cool. If you're using regular angel hair pasta, don't worry. It won't be quite the same, but no one other than me and your own Italian obsessed friend will know the difference.

While the pasta cools, make your nice, simple butter and garlic sauce. All you need to do is melt your butter over a medium heat, add your minced garlic and kosher salt, then cook the garlic for about 5 minutes, or until it starts to turn golden brown. After five minutes, quickly squeeze in your fresh lemon juice, being careful to ensure none of the bitter seeds end up in your sauce. Keep stirring for another minute, then take it off the heat.

Now, carefully arrange your cooled pasta on a serving plate or in a large oval ramekin. If you couldn't find angel hair nests, spin a generous portion of angel hair around a large fork and make a slightly curly, messy pile in the middle of a plate. You don't want the pasta to be too smooth and neat. After all, it represents her hair.

Spoon 1/6th (about a tablespoon) of the sauce over your pasta. Snuggle a peeled hard boiled egg in the middle. Go ahead and bury it in the pasta so it looks like the hair is curling all around her face. It already looks a little like River Song. To complete the effect, simply add two small slivers of black olive for the eyes and a bright stripe of roasted red bell pepper for the mouth.

A lot of diners these days are used to the thick, heavy sauces you find at chain restaurants, so you might want to double the sauce and leave the rest on the table so people can ladle more on once they start eating. Extra bell peppers and fresh black pepper also go over well, though everyone agrees they're best added after you stab poor River in the face. If you have to go zombie on anyone, hers is the no doubt the best possible brain to eat.

This recipe comes with the added bonus of having some protein in it just in case you need to test a shadow for Vashta Nerada while eating your pasta.

Sapphire Cliff Cocktail (S4E11 - Midnight)

1 shot/45 ml Bombay Sapphire gin
½ shot/22 ml blue curacao
½ shot/22 ml creme de banana
½ shot/22 ml pomegranate juice
ginger ale
banana

If, by luck, your local farmer's market, health food store, or upscale grocery happens to stock fresh blue corn, you have a perfect, easy solution to the sapphire waterfall. Simply cut the wide ends of the cobs flat before boiling then neatly arrange them like skyscrapers, surrounded by a few fallen kernels to show how rocks have succumbed to gravity over time. Since blue corn is hard to find even when it is in season, you can drown your sorrows in this Sapphire Cliff Cocktail. Fill a cocktail shaker with ice. Add the pomegranate juice, creme de banana, blue curacao, and gin (you don't have to use Bombay Sapphire, but it fits well with the name and gives you a blue rectangular bottle. Imagine the decorating uses). Top the shaker off with a handful of ice. Pound it like you're an undiscovered alien trying to beat your way into a hermetically sealed space bus.

You now have a choice. You can pour your drink into a martini glass or, if you want something to nurse for a little while, pour it into a highball glass. Either way, after you've strained the contents of your shaker into a glass, top it off with ginger ale and stir gently. Garnish the glass with a wedge of banana. After a couple of these, you'll feel like stealing the voice of the coolest person in the room.

Donna's Time Beetle (S4E12 - Turn Left)

1 large white onions
2 large red onions
3 tbsp/45 ml olive oil
3 tsp/15 g thyme
3 tsp/15 g basil
1 tsp/5 g salt
3 cloves garlic, minced

There's something on your back. It may be a time beetle, or it may be the pressure of knowing you don't have any good side dishes for your Doctor Who themed party. Either way, this easy, aromatic side dish is a great accompaniment to anything from a Tardis Wellington to Professor Yana's Gluten Neutrino Map Binder.

Let's be honest. All you're doing here is roasting onions then arranging them into the shape of a big scary beetle. It's both easy and tasty.

Preheat your oven to 425F/220C. Mix your olive oil, thyme, basil, salt, and minced garlic in a large bowl. Set that aside while you peel your onions. Cut the onions into one inch/2.5 cm wide rings. The goal here is to create a nice thick circle of oniony goodness. Cover a baking sheet with aluminum foil and spritz it generously with nonstick spray. Next, carefully dip each round cross section of your onion into the olive oil and spice mix, making sure to get both sides. Arrange each of your onion rounds on your baking sheet. When you run out of onions, bake them all for an hour.

Now comes the fun part. Find a nice serving platter. Cut two of the thickest red onion slices in half. Use the largest two halves as the top and bottom of your beetle's body. Fill in the middle with a smaller wedge of red onion to bulk up the body. Now cut one of your medium sized slices of white onion in half. Carefully arrange it at the front of your beetle to create the sharp front antenna portion of the beetle. Cut a large section of either color onion in half. Use the slices to make three legs on each side. You should have enough onions to make two beetles. Pile any excess onions onto the middle of each insect body in order to form a larger, more rounded carapace. This won't change the direction of your life for the worse, but it may change the direction of your other dishes for the better.

Dalek Invasion Ships (S4E13 - The Stolen Earth)

tube of 10 refrigerated biscuits
10 meatballs
catsup
mustard

By order of the Shadow Proclamation, this recipe is disgustingly easy. Oh, sure, you can muck about and complicate it all you want, but if you're in a bind and desperately need some kind of fast party food, you can have this on the table in 15 minutes with the added bonus of looking like you put actual work (or at least some clever thought) into it.

When we're faking it, I usually give you a real recipe I know you'll ignore (for example, Weeping Angel Wings) while also providing directions on how to make your store bought purchases look like you slaved away in a kitchen.

Not this time. We're in a rush here. People are on their way over to your apartment for an unexpected viewing party and all you have in the fridge is some biscuit dough, a bunch of random condiments, and some leftover frozen meatballs.

You'll be fine. You have everything you need to make a batch of Dalek battle ships.

If your meatballs aren't fully cooked, go ahead and cook them according to the package directions. Once they're fully cooked, spritz a baking sheet with non-stick spray and spread out each of your refrigerated biscuits so they're not touching. Cut off the bottom ⅓ of each meatball so it'll rest flatter. Now push the meatballs, cut side down, into the middle of each biscuit. Ta-da! You now have an edible old school UFO! I always pictured the Daleks in something pointier, but hey, this was the shape of their invasion fleet in the episode.

Bake the biscuits according to package directions. Having a meatball in the middle won't hurt them any more than having a Hershey's Kiss or the poached horn of a Judoon in the middle. When they're finished baking, decorate the golden brown surfaces with dots of red and yellow from the mustard and catsup. Marvel at how much these look like the actual invasion ships. You might have to load up the episode to prove it to people while they stuff their faces. It'll be a tasty surprise for everyone.

This recipe is equally good for terrorizing humans after whisking the Earth to the Medusa Cascade or coming up with a quick emergency appetizer when your usual Whovian viewing site is unavailable because an unexpected invader needs to be exterminated.

Dalek Caan's Corn (S4E14 - Journey's End)

6 fresh ears of sweet corn/maize
raisins or dried cranberries
nori
butter
salt

Admit it. Corn on the cob (maize to readers outside the United States) already kind of looks like a Dalek. All it takes is a little bit of creativity and some work with a butter knife to turn that golden corn into a crazy (yet delicious) Dalek.

Bring a large pot of water to a full boil. Once the water is merrily boiling away, dump in your half dozen ears of corn, put the lid on top, and turn off the heat. Don't move your pot. Now walk away for the next 15 minutes.

After 15 minutes, drain the corn and fill the pot with cold water. Give the corn another five to ten minutes to cool down. Once you can handle it with your bare hands, it's time to have some fun.

Cut each of your cobs down so it's only about six inches long. You want to keep the tapered top but create a nice, flat bottom so it can stand upright.

Measure about an inch from the top of your corn cob. This is your Dalek's head. For the next couple rings down, use a butter knife to loosen the kernels without removing them. Carefully cut thin strips of nori and tuck them between the loosened kernels. This will make the dark grill effect just under your Dalek's head.

Skip a ring of kernels so you have a nice, thick yellow band. Under that, cut away one entire ring of corn kernels. Fill it in with a thicker strip of Nori.

Now it's time to switch directions. Instead of going around the corn cob you're going to use the edge of your butter knife to cut straight down and remove an entire row of kernels. Leave three rows of maize, remove one row of kernels, leave three yellow rows, remove one, and continue until you've gone all the way around the cob. Replace each of the missing rows of kernels with a strip of nori. Look at the three strip wide rows of corn kernels. Go to the middle row and remove one kernel near the top. Replace it with a raisin or dried cranberry to create the Dalek's armor dots. Count down three kernels, remove one, and replace it with another bit of dried fruit. Keep going around the entire corn cob. If you don't want to use dried fruit, you can just as easily substitute nuts, miniature chocolate chips or any other small, round food of your choice.

Finally, use Pocky sticks or pretzel sticks to make your Dalek's arms and eyestalk. You'll need to get a sharp knife and cut into the cob itself in order to make the limbs stay. Alternately, you can shove a bit of pipe cleaner between some kernels for the egg beater arm and an unfolded paper clip pushed into the end of an oversized chocolate chip for the plunger arm. (Microwave the chocolate chip for 2-5 seconds to soften it first.)

Go ahead and cut the remaining corn off the discarded portions of your cobs. Put it in a bowl, top with butter and salt, and leave it discretely tucked away behind the corn Daleks for those who want to enjoy the pure flavor of corn without the admittedly odd additions of the nori and nuts or fruit.

Jackson Lake Cocktail (S4E15 - The Next Doctor)

1 shot/45 ml gin
1 cup/400 ml strong, black tea
2 tbsp/30 ml sweet orange juice
1 tsp/5 g sugar
1 tsp/5 ml maraschino cherry juice
3 drops orange bitters
1 maraschino cherry

1851 is a little early by most Steampunk standards, but that didn't stop the prop department from cramming this episode full of gears.

There was a certain temptation to go crazy with heavy, fatty recipes topped with gear shaped crusts, but that's material for another cookbook. I really wanted to make Cyberman cinnamon pull-apart brain bread decorated with aluminum foil faces and antenna. While that resulted in many delicious experiments, in the end none of them looked enough like a Cyberman for my tastes. Feel free to give it a try, though.

I also toyed with the idea of a "Tardis" hot air balloon mezze plate, but that ended up looking more like it belonged at a kid's uninspired birthday party than at a dinner full of ambitious Whovians.

After two failed experiments, I realized what this episode really needed was a good, stiff drink.

Brew a cup of strong black tea. If you're a regular tea drinker, just add a couple of lumps. If you're not, add a teaspoon of sugar. Stir well until the sugar is fully dissolved.

Now add the gin, for England's most popular spirit of the mid 19th century. Soften the flavor with the orange juice, and maraschino cherry juice. Finish the drink off with three shakes of orange bitters to represent Jackson Lake's tears.

You can either serve it warm in a comforting mug or you can pour everything into a cocktail shaker full of ice, pound the shaker like a weeping man who has lost his memories, and strain it into a martini glass. (Americans who enjoy iced tea are likely to appreciate the later version.) Either way, garnish the glass with a fresh maraschino cherry and enjoy.

Squash Stingrays (S4E16 - Planet of the Dead)

1 head of red cabbage
3 medium yellow squash, halved and seeds removed
6 large, fresh basil leaves
1 cup/226 g cream cheese
1/2/113 g cup sour cream
2 tbsp/30 g Herbes de Provence (or your favorite herb mix)
1 tsp/5 g kosher salt
1/2 tsp/2.5 g fresh cracked black pepper

Skate (a relative of stingrays) immediately came to mind when I saw those flying stingray spaceships. However, skate is expensive, tricky to cook, and unless your guests are experts at identifying cooked fish, the final product won't be instantly recognizable as something from a Doctor Who episode. Those of you who like inside jokes (and are very good at cooking delicate fish) are welcome to give it a try anyway. The rest of us will be over here in a corner making silly stingray shaped spaceships out of yellow squash.

You get a pretty good bang for your buck with these vegetarian spaceships. Slice each yellow squash in half, lengthwise. Use a spoon to neatly scoop out all the seeds. This process also happens to create your ship's command center. Line the cabin with a fresh basil leaf.

In a separate bowl, mix your room temperature cream cheese, sour cream, Herbs de Provence (or generic Italian seasoning if you don't like the hint of lavender), salt, and pepper until they're well blended. Equally divide the mix between the six cockpits.

Arrange them cockpit side up on a baking sheet and pop them in a 350F/178C oven for 25-35 minutes, or until the squash's flesh is fork tender.

While the squash is baking, carefully remove the leaves off your purple cabbage. Once the squash is done, you can arrange the squash ships on a plate and start making the stingray-esque wings.

I like to flesh this out with some of the Hath slaw from Series 7, The Doctor's Daughter. Carefully pile it alongside the squash in a vague wing shape. Take the cabbage leaves you removed and trim them into the shape of flappy stingray wings and arrange them over the slaw. If you don't feel like making slaw, don't worry. You can just pile up a few layers of cut purple cabbage until you achieve the thickness and shape of a stingray wing on each side, and just treat the purple cabbage as a garnish. Either way, you end up with a tasty, edible spaceship that looks like it should be zooming around a doomed planet.

The Fizzy Waters of Mars Cocktail (S4E17 - The Waters of Mars)

1 shot/45 ml pomegranate liqueur
1 shot/45 ml ginger ale
2 lime wedges
pink Champagne or sparkling wine

It was tempting to simply tell people to fill their mouths with red pop rocks and ginger ale for this one. Then I remembered that was explosively disgusting, albeit nicely dramatic.

In honor of Earth's first extra terrestrial colony, I present the Fizzy Waters of Mars cocktail. Drinking one probably won't kill you, but drinking six will leave you hung over the next morning, feeling like your body is being inhabited by aliens determined to suck all the moisture from your body.

Simply pour the ginger ale and pomegranate liqueur into a champagne flute. Top the flute off with pink champagne. Squeeze in the juice of one lime wedge to give it some bite and garnish the glass with the other.

The Master's Drums (S4E18 - The End of Time)

4 cups/720 g prepared macaroni and cheese
8 rounds of puff pastry
nori
butter

Some episodes, coming up with a recipe is a challenge. This one was just the opposite. Oh, the wealth of ideas. You could host an entire party based on this alone. The tentacle faced Ood practically beg for recipes. The Cactus people are ripe with potential. The Seal of Rassilon belongs on a pizza. Heck, The Master spends half the episode wolfing down everything from an entire chicken, gristle and all, to the contents of an entire food truck (including the staff.) To cap it all off, the episode takes place at Christmas and ends with The Doctor's regeneration. So much ripe potential! How to choose? In the end, I decided to go with the Master's Drums. They're beating in his head through the whole series, and if anything deserves a crazy homage, they qualify.

Make whatever kind of macaroni and cheese you most enjoy. If yours normally comes out of a certain blue box loved by kids, I won't tell. You're just as welcome to make it from scratch using the fanciest of cheeses. The real point is you should use something you like. However, if you do decide to go with the blue box macaroni and cheese, you'll need to add about ½ cup of actual shredded yellow cheese as a binder. This needs to be pretty sticky.

Once you've prepared your macaroni and cheese, grease up eight round, straight edged ramekins. You want to really butter the heck out of the insides. Otherwise, your drums won't come out evenly. Use your ramekins as a cookie cutter and cut out sixteen nice, neat circular discs in your puff pastry. Slide one into the bottom of each ramekin. Now fill the ramekins up with macaroni and cheese. Pack it in there nice and tight. (Remember, if you used the blue box stuff, add some extra cheese to glue all the noodles together.) However tight you think is enough, use the edge of a buttered spoon and pack it in tighter. Now cram the second disc of puff pastry on top.

Bake the drums at 350F/178C for 20 minutes, or until the tops are a dark, golden brown. Once the drums are finished, let them cool for at least 10 (preferably 20) minutes before messing with them. Trust me. If you don't let the cheese set as it cools, you'll end up with nothing but an uneven pile of sticky noodles. Once the drums have cooled, use a thin rubber spatula to loosen the edges. Carefully upend each drum onto a platter. Cut a sheet of Nori the same thickness as your drum and quickly wrap it around the macaroni and cheese. Once each of your cheese drums is wrapped, get a very sharp knife and carefully cut thin lines along the sides to represent the drum's support struts.

You should end up with a set of eight edible macaroni and cheese drums. Eating them won't offset the horrible pounding that's plagued you since childhood, but they will briefly help curb the insatiable hunger from your failed regeneration.

SERIES 5: THE GIRL WHO WAITED

The New Doctor's Rubbish Plate (S5E1 - The Eleventh Hour)

apples
yogurt (with bits in)
bacon
beans
bread and butter
carrots (he knows they're rubbish without even trying)

Admit it. You're expecting fish fingers and custard. Of course you are. Everyone loves fish fingers and custard. That's why I have a whole chapter dedicated to it. Meanwhile, let's take a look at all the other things the brand new eleventh Doctor finds total rubbish. A new mouth is confusing.

The sliced apples, carrots, and yogurt with bits in actually go together pretty well. People serve fruit and veggies with yogurt dip all the time

You can either pile everything into bowls so they can sit on the same platter, or set up two adjacent platters with a symbolically carved apple on each one so people know they belong together.

If you're going for two platters, slice the apples (squirt lemon juice over them to keep them from browning) and arrange the apple slices, carrots, and yogurt on one plate. Put the beans, bacon, and bread and butter on another. This is hands down, one of the fastest and simplest things you can serve your guests. Make sure both plates have one whole apple with a smiley face carved into one side.

If you're feeling extra schmancy you can always surround the rubbish with a baked eel in jelly as a stand in for the multiform that lives upstairs from Amy Pond, but that requires you to actually like eel. If you do, the recipes in this book probably seem downright mundane.

Confidentially, if you want to sexy this up with the addition of an Atraxi spaceship you can always cut one of those giant eyeball shaped gumballs in half (available in both candy stores and in gumball machines near the exit of many groceries.) Get some pre-made sugar cookie dough. Roll it out, cut it into a big spikey snow flake, and suddenly you have an Atraxi spaceship. Bake the sugar cookie according to package directions. While the cookie is still warm, squish the sliced eyeball into the middle of the spaceship and let it cool into place. Position it in one corner of the plate so it can creepily watch everyone eat.

Alternately, if you're Scottish, you can just fry something.

Bow Tie Pasta with Protesting Star Whale Brains (S5E2 - The Beast Below)

1 lb/450 g bow tie pasta
4 tbsp/60 ml olive oil
1 lb/450 g cherry tomatoes
1 medium red onion, diced
4 cloves of garlic, minced
6 large fresh basil leaves ripped into small pieces
3 tbsp/45 g pine nuts
1 tsp/5 g salt
1 tsp/5 g fresh ground black pepper
1 lb/450 g of prepared meatballs or your favorite cooked
sausage cut into 1 inch chunks
juice of 1 lemon

Any fully prepared Doctor Who theme party has to include
glasses of water on the floor. While you cook, remind your
guests to watch the glasses for vibrations.

This is another one of those mildly steampunky episodes that made me want to slap gears and keys and unnecessarily intricate locks onto random foods. Instead, in honor of The Doctor's new look, this is an excuse to whip out some bow tie pasta, because everyone knows bow ties are cool.

Confidentially, I was stupidly excited when I found red bow tie pasta online. I was sure it would be perfect for this recipe. In reality, boiling the pasta leeched out most of the color. Instead of red bow ties, I had these sort of anemic grey ones that looked like the sort of fashion statement you'd expect from the Silents.

If you find red bow tie pasta, feel free to give it a try. You may stumble across some higher quality stuff than what I found. Just to be safe, though pick up a box of the regular stuff while you're at it. If your dyed pasta bleeds out, the bright red cherry tomatoes will give the bow ties lots of color. Don't stress over it.

Slice your cherry tomatoes in half. They'll be pretty darn wet, so let them sit and drain in a colander. While the tomatoes are draining, cook the pasta according to package directions.

As the pasta merrily boils away, cook the onions and garlic in one tablespoon of oil. Once they've started to brown, empty them into a large mixing bowl. Don't clean your skillet. Instead, return it to a medium heat and add the pine nuts. Stir quickly, gently browning them. Pine nuts have a nasty habit of going from golden brown to horribly burned shockingly fast, so keep a close eye on them. They should be done in 3-4 minutes. Empty them into the same bowl with the onions.

By now, your pasta should be finished cooking. Drain it, rinse it with cool water, and set it aside while you finish mixing up the rest of the sauce. Add the rest of the olive oil, the juice of one lemon (make sure to strain out the seeds), your salt, pepper, ripped basil leaves and drained cherry tomato halves to the sautéed onions and garlic. Give it all a good, hearty stir. Once everything is well blended, add the drained bowtie pasta and mix it all together until the pasta is well coated.

If you chose to protest, you can now add some pre cooked meatballs or your choice of pre-cooked (pink, brainy looking) sausage to represent the Star Whale brains. If you're a vegetarian, or you chose to forget, leave it a clean, meat free dish that merely celebrates the inherent coolness of bowties.

Before you let people dive into the dish, make sure they either Protest or Forget your party. It's for their protection. After all, this could be a wild night.

Open Faced Dalek Ironsides (S5E3 - Victory of the Daleks)

15 cherry tomatoes grown in your home victory garden
4 slices national loaf
4 slices bacon
4 leaves of lettuce
2 tbsp/30 ml mayonnaise
1 tbsp/15 g fresh basil or other garden herbs

Oh, look. A new Dalek paradigm. Because Skaro, Dalek Sek, and the pig people weren't enough. This time, though, the biggest Dalek innovation is that they suddenly come in candy colors!

Don't worry. You're not getting an M&M's themed Dalek recipe. Instead, in the spirit of this episode, we're using authentic World War II ingredients to make a surprisingly Dalek-tastic sandwich.

Churchill may have been a stout man, but everyone serving under him was on strict, austere rations. Luckily for you, this wartime austerity sandwich will fill your belly while also evoking the new Ironsides.

Cut your cherry tomatoes in half and let them sit in a colander to drain. I know you're thinking of skipping this step, but if you do, the moisture in your tomatoes will exterminate the structural stability of your bread. While the tomatoes drain, mix two tablespoons of mayonnaise with whatever herbs you grow in your victory garden (fresh basil is nice, but you're also welcome to use one teaspoon of your favorite mixed dried herbs, such as thyme, or dill).

Now slice your bacon in half length-wise so you now have eight very thin slices. Fry up your bacon until it's nice and crispy. You can't waste something as precious as cooking fat, so fry up your slices of national loaf (or whatever brown bread you have lying about) in the bacon grease.

Once all your bread is nice and crispy, cut the top, rounded third off two slices. Arrange whole slices directly above them. Between the curved top and the long, tapered body, you can already start to see a Dalek taking shape. Four slices is enough bread for two Dalek sandwiches.

Spread the slices of bread with a thin layer of the mayo mix. Lay one thin slice of bacon horizontally just beneath the top crust of the bread. Beneath that, lay down three slices of bacon in neat rows. Arrange the cherry tomato halves on top of the lower bacon slices so you have a neat grid of shiny Dalek-armor dots. A single round slice of olive makes a good eyeball stalk substitute. You can make some arms from a broken Pocky stick and a snipped cotton swab.

If you've used up your entire meat ration for the week or you happen to be a vegetarian time traveler, you can omit the bacon (or substitute Morningstar Farms soy bacon) and just toast the bread.

Once you have Dalek shaped sandwiches, arrange the lettuce leaves like a garnish.

If you don't want to eat these open faced, simply stack an extra slice of toast underneath each of the Dalek's body segments. When someone dissects the Dalek to callously eat the body, they can simply toss the lettuce on top of the tomatoes, flip the extra slice of bread on top, and chow down on what would've been a hearty and decadent sandwich during WWII.

These Dalek Ironside sandwiches are best served with tea, jammy dodgers, and a threat of extermination.

Irradiated Angels (S5E4 - The Time of Angels)

1.5 cups/200 g flour
1.5 cups/200 g sugar
1.5 tsp/7.5 g baking powder
3/4 tsp/4 g salt
6 tbsp/90 g room temperature, unsalted butter
3/4 cup/100 g unsweetened cocoa powder
3 large eggs
1 tsp/5 g vanilla
1 cup/200 g semisweet chocolate chips (may use miniature chips)
3/4 cup/100 g powdered sugar

I was immensely tempted to whip up a recipe for hallucinogenic lipstick. After all, lip balm is surprisingly easy to make with little more than Vaseline and Kool-Aid. Add some hallucinogens and you're well on your way to pretending to be River Song - or possibly getting yourself arrested. Wait, that's part of being River Song.

Since The Doctor doesn't come to my rescue whenever I write "Hello Sweetie" on a random wall, I decided to go with something less criminal-tastic for this recipe. Instead, the crackled surface of these cookies resemble the irradiated angels onboard the *Byzantium*. Don't blink while you eat them or else you risk ending up like Angel Bob.

Combine the flour, baking powder, sugar, and salt in a large bowl. In another bowl, mix the butter and cocoa powder until you have a smooth paste. Add the vanilla and eggs then give it a good stir. Now, mix the dry ingredients into the wet ingredients.

I know what you're thinking. The mix doesn't seem anywhere near moist enough. You're wrong. Use your hands and really dig in there to mix it all up. Eventually, it'll end up the same consistency as a very thick brownie batter. Once it does, fold in the chocolate chips and try to get them as evenly distributed as possible.

Put the batter in the fridge and let it sit for about half an hour. This is a good time to go watch an episode of Doctor Who. Don't worry. The batter will be just fine if you end up waiting 45 minutes. Heck, you could do a four hour marathon without harming the batter.

When you come back, preheat your oven to 350F/178C. Grease the heck out of two baking sheets. Put your powdered sugar in a bowl. Now you're ready to make some angels. If you have an angel shaped cookie cutter, roll out your dough, cut it into angel shapes, dip the shapes lightly in powdered sugar, and arrange them on your cookie sheets.

If you don't have an angel shaped cookie cutter, make rough oval balls from the batter, use your fingers to pinch a nose, push in some eyes, and slice in a mouth, then also lightly dunk them into the baking powder before putting the cookies on your baking sheets. It may look crude, but really, as long as you have a face, you'll be fine.

Bake the cookies for 12-15 minutes, depending on their size. They'll spread a bit and puff out, which creates the cracked, aged surface you want in an irradiated angel. The longer you cook them, the crunchier they get.

Let each batch cool for about 10 minutes so they'll solidify. Once they've hardened, use a spatula to gently remove them from the cookie sheet and get to baking your next batch.

These cookies are incredibly forgiving. After all, you want your bodies to look rough and weather beaten. If you happen to have an angel shaped cookie cutter, these look awesome arranged in an angry circle surrounding one of your Tardis toys.

Angel Wing Cookies (S5E5 - Flesh and Stone)

1 cup/230 g cold butter, cubed
1.5 cups/200 g flour
1/2 cup/115 g sour cream
10 tbsp/150 g sugar
3 tsp/15 g ground cinnamon

Human beings are incredible omnivores. We'll eat darn near anything that isn't a rock - and if the rock is made of salt, we'll make an exception. Unsurprisingly, it's not easy to make food that looks like stones.

These classic cookies have a coarse, rough hewn texture that, if you squint right after a couple drinks, will remind you a little of cheap rock. While you're drunkenly squinting, remind yourself that they're also wing shaped.

To get started, make your life easier by cutting your butter into cubes. Toss the butter cubes and your flour into a large bowl and use your fingers to mash them together until you end up with a buttery mix that looks like coarse crumbs. This is deliciousness in the making. Now dump in your sour cream and give it an enthusiastic stir. The flour and butter should absorb the sour cream pretty quickly, giving you an actual dough. Knead it together about half a dozen times to make sure it all holds together.

Once you have achieved a solid, shape the dough into four balls and flatten them slightly. Wrap your balls in plastic wrap and put them in the fridge for at least four hours. You can always leave the cookie dough overnight and come back the next day. Whenever you're ready, sprinkle a sheet of waxed paper with two tablespoons of sugar. Unwrap one of your dough balls and just roll it around on the sugar until it's nicely coated. Put another piece of waxed paper on top and get out your rolling pin. If you don't have a rolling pin, get your largest canned goods. It really doesn't matter what you use as long as you roll the dough into a big 12 x 5 inch (30.5 x 13 cm) rectangle. Sprinkle your rectangle with 1 teaspoon/5 grams of cinnamon.

Now for the fun part. When I was a kid, I thought each of these cookies had to be individually rolled into shape. Learning this trick was like baking magic. Start at the short end of the dough and roll it towards the middle, like you're making a jelly roll. Stop halfway. Go to the other end and roll it towards the middle in the same way. The dough should meet as two spirals linked in the middle. Look at it from the side and you can already see it looking a little like wings.

Wrap the dough in plastic. To make the dough look more wing-like, pinch the edges of each "wing" into a point and poke the shoulders (where the two spirals are connected by a single layer of dough) downwards a little to make the curve of the back. Put your dough in the freezer for half an hour. This is just enough time for you to repeat the process on the other three lumps of dough waiting in your fridge.

While you're waiting half an hour, preheat your oven to 375F/190C and pour your remaining sugar into a saucer or a shallow plate. Don't leave the dough in the freezer too long. You just want to firm it up a bit so the cookies will hold their shape when sliced.

Take the wings out of the freezer after 30 minutes. Unwrap your first one and cut it into ½ inch/1.25 centimeter slices. Each slice should look like you cut it off the back of a weeping angel. Dip the cookies into sugar and put them onto an ungreased baking sheet at least 2 inches apart. Angels need their personal space.

Bake for 12 minutes, or until golden brown. Take the cookies out of the oven, briefly admire your handiwork, then flip them over and put them right back in the oven for another 5-8 minutes.

If you're feeling whimsical, you can also make some appropriately sized triangular (for the body and skirt) and round (for the head) sugar cookies then arrange them into angel shapes on a plate. Alternately, you can add just a couple drops of black food coloring to the sour cream before mixing it in. This will give the dough a more grey color, which, with the crystalline texture of the sugar, enhances the stone-like appearance. Experience says making grey dough will also put people off your cookies, because our reptile brains can't get past the grey crunchy look in order to appreciate the buttery goodness within. It's your call.

Vampire Space Fish (S5E6 - The Vampires of Venice)

1 lb/455 g of cod fillets (or other whitefish of your choice)
2 tomatoes, diced
1 red bell pepper, diced
½ onion, diced
2 cloves of garlic, minced
2 tbsp/30 g butter
1 tbsp/15 g flour
1 tsp/5 g honey
½ tsp/2.5 g salt
½ tsp/2.5 g marjoram
½ tsp/2.5 g basil
¼ tsp/1 g thyme
2 sheets puff pastry, defrosted
2 eggs, beaten
1 ball of aluminum foil
1 set of plastic fake vampire teeth

The first time I saw this episode, I knew I was going to make some kind of gigantic bitey fish dish. The obvious answer here would be a giant, bone-in fish with big honking teeth. Sadly, I'm part grossed out by eating fish with eyes. They always seem to be watching me, judging me, critical of my choice of sauce. Not this time.

Preheat your oven to 425F/218C. While your oven warms up, toss your butter in a skillet and melt it over a medium-high heat. Throw in your diced onion and sauté until it starts to turn translucent. Add in the garlic and bell peppers and continue to cook the mix until the onions just start to brown. Now throw in your nice juicy diced tomatoes along with your salt, marjoram, basil, thyme, and honey. Give it all a good stir. It should be a bit liquidy in there. Continue cooking for another two minutes, then sprinkle a tablespoon of flour on top. This will thicken up the sauce a little so you don't soak through your puff pastry while it cooks. If it still looks too wet, add another tablespoon of flour.

Take the filling off the heat and get ready for the fishy fun part. Put one piece of puff pastry on a greased baking sheet. Arrange your cod filets vaguely into the shape of a fish. Top the filets with your bloody red, organic, meaty looking tomato mix. These are vampire space fish, after all. You need a little red in there. Now lay your second sheet of puff pastry on top and pinch it down around the edges of your vague fishy shape. Cut away the excess puff pastry. You now have a crude fish loaf stuffed with actual fish. It's a good start, but you can do better. Pinch the edges around everything but the mouth. When it comes to the mouth, mash up a ball of aluminum foil about the same size as your plastic vampire teeth. Shove it in where the mouth should go.

See all that leftover puff pastry? You can't waste something like that. Use a beer bottle cap or very small cookie cutter to cut it into the shape of scales, then carefully arrange the scales across the top of your fish's body. You can use other scraps to create fins or tail details if you're feeling fancy. If you couldn't find any plastic vampire teeth, create an oversized dough mouth then cut the puff pastry scraps into lots of long, sharp pointy teeth and use them to fill the mouth with razor-like goodness. When you're done decorating your fish, whisk up two eggs until they're slightly frothy. Use a pastry brush to coat the whole fish with a light layer of egg. That'll give it a lovely shine and help it bake up into a pretty golden brown.

Lightly tent some aluminum foil over your evil space fish and pop it in the oven for 15 minutes. Remove the aluminum foil and bake it for another 20 minutes. You want to make sure it's in the oven long enough for the fish to bake all the way through but not so long that you burn the puff pastry.

If you opted for the big fake teeth, as soon as you take the fish out of the oven, carefully remove the aluminum foil plug and shove the plastic teeth in there instead. You may have to do a little strategic squishing. If you left too big a gap, you can always fill it in with some white cheese to match the color of the plastic teeth.

Serve the fish with a side of Donna's Time Beetle, a hearty glass of red wine, and a reminder to your single female guests that at least they're not being fed to thousands of piranha-like husbands after dinner.

Ledweth's Eknodine Pensioners (S5E7 - Amy's Choice)

baby cucumbers
nori
leftover Slitheen Eggs
olive slices or edible googly eyes
toothpicks
red food coloring

Based on the start of this episode, I know you're expecting something based on Amy's pregnancy baking spree - a cake, or maybe some muffins. However, it's hard to resist the lure of the crazy Eknodine in Rory's fantasy world. They're an instantly recognizable alien that happens to be easy to make. Hold one of these in your mouth and have fun freaking out your guests.

To make your own Eknodine, start by cutting a three inch/7.5 centimeter slit into one end of your baby cucumber, length wise.

Turn it 180 degrees and cut a second slit. You should now have four sort of tentacles sticking out of one end of your cucumber. Carve out a little of the white interior. Now use a knife to cut each of the four wedges into several smaller wispy tentacles. You'll need to carve out more of the white meat of the cucumber in order to make room for the eye shaped egg.

Once you have the mouth complete, cut a wide circle of nori and push it into the middle of the hole. This is just to add to some fullness to the mouth. If you don't have nori around the house, don't worry. Now shove the egg into the nest of tentacles, pointy side facing down into the meat of the cucumber. Use a couple of toothpicks to secure the peeled Slitheen egg in place. Try to pierce one of the fleshier tentacles, go through the egg, and come out a fleshy tentacles on the other side. The good thing about this is the actual Eknodine had all kinds of spiky bits, so the toothpicks actually add to the overall effect. Feel free to have some pinning down every tentacle.

Finish it off by cutting an olive shaped circle into the eye and pushing the olive round into place to make the pupil. Alternately, just use a googly eye from the cake decorating aisle of your grocery store. Squeeze one drop of red food coloring into the middle of the pupil and let it drip around the eye to give it a good bloodshot look.

If you do this right, you should have something sturdy enough for you to hold one end in your mouth without it all falling apart. Enjoy blowing some powdered sugar in people's faces before menacing them with a mouthful of something that looks like it should be fighting Sigourney Weaver.

Silurian Hot House Salad with Lemon-Lime Vinaigrette (S5E8 - The Hungry Earth)

Salad:
4 cups/170 grams salad greens
1 Clementine or Satsuma orange
1 red bell pepper
½ cucumber

Dressing:
1 tbsp/15 ml olive oil
¼ cup/60 ml white vinegar
½ cup/120 ml water
1 lemon
1 lime
½ tsp/2.5 g salt
½ tsp/2.5 g sugar

Oh, baby. It's so hot down here, 22 miles beneath the surface of the Earth. In honor of the green Silurian scales and the red blood spilled in their unnecessary conflict, I present this hot house salad. Making a salad isn't complicated. Peel your orange and break it into segments. Cut half of your cucumber into thin slices. Seed your bell pepper and cut it into thin strips. Spread your spinach over a nice platter and artistically arrange the cucumber, orange, and pepper slices on top.

To make the dressing, carefully juice your lemon and lime, making sure to filter out any seeds. Pour the juice and all the other ingredients into a clean jar or plastic ware container and shake it like the earth just mysteriously moved under your feet. Keep shaking it until everything inside is so mixed up it the ingredients aren't sure what timeline they're stuck in. Lightly drizzle the result over the top of the salad.

Cinnamon Pull Apart Crack in the Wall (S5E9 - Cold Blood)

4 packages of generic cinnamon roll dough
pre-made refrigerated sugar cookie dough
butter
parchment paper
an action figure of Rory

The second time I watched this episode, I knew I had to make that man eating crack in the wall. The first time, I was too busy shouting at my television, "Give Rory back!" When I decided I wanted to pay homage to Rory's second death in the span of three episodes, that rugged brown wall with the gaping white light seemed so easy to reproduce.I was wrong.

First, I tried making it a main dish. Layers of seasoned ground beef were transformed into thick ropes, which I then stacked on top of one another to make the wall. It could stand in a puddle of alfredo sauce to represent the gushing light with a crack shaped cheese wedge stuffed into the middle. Except, of course, after multiple tries I just couldn't get it out of the pan and arranged upright without the whole affair falling apart. You're welcome to try. I'd love to see a photo and read your recipe if you can make it work

Instead, I decided to go with my second choice, cinnamon pull-apart bread.

The batch of homemade bread tasted nice, but didn't quite have the layered wood look I was hoping for. Then it hit me. This is supposed to be an easy cookbook for Whovians who just want to throw a fun party. I was making this way too difficult.

Part of me is ashamed to admit I even tried this, but even my inner foodie has to admit this is fast, easy, impressive, and cheap. You can make the whole thing for less than $10.

The great thing about cheap generic cinnamon roll dough is that it's already arranged in neat rectangles. It's amazing how much that stuff already looks like the beams of a rough hewn wooden wall.

To complete the transformation, line a dish with parchment paper for easy removal and yes, use some butter to grease the heck out of the paper. Remember that you're baking your wall flat. It needs to come out and stand up to achieve the full effect (propping it against a cardboard box works best). Starting at the bottom of your pan, stack the long rectangles of dough on top of one another to build the base of the wall.

About ⅓ of the way from the bottom, pause and get out your sugar cookie dough. You should've picked this up at the grocery store while you were grabbing four freaking cans of cinnamon rolls and dodging questions about courting type two diabetes. Cut out a thick wedge and use your fingers to sculpt it into a rough crack in the wall shape. By the time it absorbed Rory, the crack was pretty big. For our purposes, you want it to stretch about3/4 of the way across the width of the wall. If it goes any further than that, you'll lose structural integrity.

Once your crack is in place, start filling in the rest of the wall using your remaining rectangles of cinnamon roll dough. Squish them in nice and tight, right on top of one another.

This will need to bake a little longer than your average pan of cinnamon rolls, but not as much longer as you probably think. I found mine was good after adding about four minutes to the package directions. Try adding four minutes to the time on your dough, then start checking every two minutes until your wall is a dark, golden brown.

Once it comes out, your lovely white sugar cookie will be a dark golden brown. Use the edge of a very sharp knife to cut the brown surface off. Now fill the cavity with some of the pure white icing that comes with your cinnamon rolls.

This is very important. Now you have to leave it the heck alone. Your carefully made wall really needs to cool completely or else it'll fall apart. This is a good time to go watch any of the episodes where Rory is a sexy Roman.

After half an hour or more, use the parchment paper to carefully lift the wall out of the baking pan. Prop the wall against a brown cardboard box to keep it upright. (The brown cardboard also creates the illusion your wall is in a cave, just like in the episode.) Empty the rest of your icing in front of the wall to represent the light spilling from the crack. The base of your wall should appear to be swimming in white light. If you have any fake ivy or leaves around the house, feel free to decorate the box. This wall had a very organic look.

Complete the effect with a Rory Williams action figure curled up at the edge of the icing pool.

Vincent's Rustic Potatoes (S5E10 - Vincent and the Doctor)

1/2 cup/115 g butter
3 lbs/1400 g white russet potatoes, peeled
1.5 lbs/680 g purple potatoes, peeled
1lb/450 g yams, peeled
1 3/4 tsp/8.75 g salt
1/2 tsp/2.5 g ground black pepper
1 tbsp/15 ml olive oil

This is one of my favorite character episodes. They don't dance around Vincent's troubles, nor do they save him from his early death, but they do let a depressed, impoverished artist know that he mattered.

Like most poor people in France, Vincent's diet would've revolved around potatoes. Therefore, I present this slightly modified version of the classic French dish, Potatoes Anna. In honor of the Tardis, I've switched up the colors to include purple potatoes and bright orange yams. In honor of Vincent, this is best served with a cheap bottle of rough red wine and some scraps of chicken stolen from someone else's plate.

Start by preheating your oven to 425F/218C. While the oven is merrily heating away, melt your butter in a small saucepan until it's nice and foamy. Then, because you're a fickle artist, skim off the foam.

While the butter melts, peel all your potatoes. Cut them into nice, ⅛ inch slices and arrange them into an overlapping pattern in a round cake pan or oven safe skillet. As you finish one layer, brush it with melted butter and sprinkle with ½ tsp of salt. Keep adding layers, buttering and salting between each one, until you run out of potatoes. Feel free to alternate thick layers of white with thinner layers of blue and orange.

If you're good with a knife, make sure your top layer is white, ring it with the orange sweet potatoes (possibly cut into Dalek shapes) and use the purple potatoes to make either a Tardis or a giant DW sigil in the middle of the pan. If you're feeling inspired by all that blue, you can also try to make a sort of starry night pattern. If you're not a troubled artist working in an underappreciated medium, stick with dramatic rings of colors.

You want to compact this as tightly as possible, so once you're out of potatoes, press down hard with a skillet. If you have another heavy pan that fits inside the first (like a smaller cast iron skillet) push it down hard to flatten the potatoes as much as possible. Seriously. Really squish them in there.

Once squished, finish the top layer by pouring on the last of the butter and sprinkling the top with fresh ground black pepper and your remaining salt.

Tent some aluminum foil over the top. Put the whole thing in the oven and bake it for 50 minutes. Remove the aluminum foil, crank the temperature up to 500F/260C, and bake for 10 more minutes or until the edges turn nice and golden.

When it's done, let your dish sit and cool for about 10 minutes. Run a rubber or silicone spatula around the edges to loosen it up. Enjoy it with a bottle of cheap red wine, some toasted sunflower seeds, and a painful appreciation of all the colors in the night sky.

The Doctor's Omelet (S5E11 - The Lodger)

2 eggs
2 tbsp/30 ml milk
1 tsp/5 g Herbes de Provence
½ tsp/2.5 g salt
½ tsp/2.5 g fresh ground black pepper
⅓ cup/100 g fresh grated hard parmesan cheese
4 slices of whatever lunchmeat is in your fridge
mayonnaise
butter

I'll be honest. I'm a little dubious about The Doctor's cooking skills. Sure, Craig says this is the best omelet he's ever tasted, but I've never started breakfast by dumping whole eggs into a cold pan and swirling them around with what looks like some lunch meat scraps.

You're welcome to try it his way. I, not being a Time Lord, mucked about with the order a bit and, since he said he learned to cook in Paris, added a bit of Herbes de Provence. This omelet is best served with strong black tea drunk straight from the pot, full of "excited tannin molecules."

Crack the eggs into a bowl Add the milk, salt, pepper, and Herbes de Provence. Whisk it all together with a slightly manic enthusiasm.

The next step is important. This is where nearly ever failed omelet went wrong. Put a smallish nonstick skillet on a medium heat. No hotter - I mean it! Medium. Now enthusiastically butter the interior of your skillet. For a proper omelet, your nonstick skillet still needs some edible lubrication.

Now that you have a buttery, medium-warm skillet, pour in your egg mix, tilt the skillet so it spreads evenly along the bottom, then leave it the heck alone. Walk away if you have to.

In 3-4 minutes, your egg should be set, which means the interior will still look a little bit soft and runny while the edges have turned golden brown. Rip up your lunch meat and spread it across one half of the omelet. Top that with your parmesan cheese. Now oh so carefully use a spatula (two, if you don't have much practice) to flip the bare half of your omelet on top of the lunchmeat coated side. Don't panic if you didn't get an exact seal. You'll be fine. In fact, if you didn't make it in one piece, just layer it on as best you can and try to neaten things up a little.

For your next trick, slide the omelet onto a plate. If your top half is kind of messy, put two plates together, flip it over, and presto, your nice, neat bottom half is now on top. You look like a pro at this.

The Doctor squirted a rather intimidating amount of mayonnaise right in the pan along with the whole eggs. I suggest you, not being a Time Lord, merely make an artistic dab along one side of the plate and let your guests decide how much of the condiment they want to enjoy with their omelet. Not everyone is as blindly accepting as Craig.

Omelets are fast, easy, and cheap. Confidentially, you can always make one true to the episode plus some more edible omelets for your vegetarian guests. Roasted red bell pepper strips, spinach, and crumbled goat cheese go together really well, as do fresh garlic, fresh basil leaves, and fresh green onions. Historically, omelets have been served as a main course any time of day, and were usually stuffed with whatever leftovers people had around the house, so just have fun with it.

In honor of the trapped Tardis, serve this garnished with a handful of blueberries and an electronic toothbrush.

Rory the Roman's Farro Stew (S5E12 - The Pandorica Opens)

2 tbsp/30ml olive oil
2 leeks, white parts only, sliced
1 1/2 cups/300 g pearl farro
6 cups/1.4 l beef broth
1 tsp/5 g salt
1 tsp/5 g fresh ground black pepper
2 tbsp/30 g crumbled goat cheese

I'll be honest with you here. My first impulse was to make a Stonehenge sculpture out of hot dogs with one of my white chocolate and strawberry Cyberman heads inside. Heck, you could surround your MeatHenge with two of every alien, as though you were creating the scariest ark in the universe.

Then I saw Rory - the first man to be totally unimpressed when he walked onto the Tardis - and decided to honor him and the rest of his plastic legionnaires with this hearty, simple ancient Roman stew.

You can find farro at most health food stores, schmancy groceries, and even on Amazon. If you're in a pinch, go ahead and substitute pearl barley. The flavor will be a little different, but the Romans were pretty flexible. They came. They saw. They conquered. Along the way, they ate whatever they could get their hot Italian hands on.

To make this simple, hearty legionnaires stew, start by putting a soup pot on a medium heat and adding your olive oil and leeks. Cook for 7-10 minutes, or until the leeks are golden brown. Now simply add everything but the cheese. Give it a good stir and put a lid on the stew. Wait for it to come to a boil. Give it one more enthusiastic stir, turn the heat down to low, and put the lid back on. Leave it alone for the next hour and half, or until the farro has absorbed a lot of the moisture and become nice and tender. You'll naturally want to peek, but try not to take off the lid and stir the stew more often than every 15 minutes.

Once the stew is finished, ladle it into bowls, drizzle a little extra olive oil on top, then finish each bowl with a sprinkle of goat cheese and a dash of salt and pepper. The salt would've been expensive for Romans, but after a visit by Caesar and Cleopatra up near Londinium, surely the wealthy guests would've spread a little wealth around for the soldiers.

This is best served with hearty, homemade bread, whatever seasonal vegetables you can scavenge, and a hearty sense of cultural superiority

The Pond's Wedding Punch (S5E13 - The Big Bang)

8 cups/2 l water
1 cup/237 ml vodka
1 cup/200 g sugar
4 cups/520 g fresh blueberries
1.5 cups/355 ml fresh squeezed lemon juice
2 lemons, sliced into wheels
zest of 1 lemon
blue sugar (optional)
blue food coloring (optional)

After 2000 years of waiting, Rory finally got the girl. You were probably expecting a Tardis shaped cake in celebration of Amy and Rory's wedding. Hey, you didn't plunk down cold hard cash for a recipe you can find anywhere on the internet. You want something bold, something different, something full of spoilers. This recipe gets you two of the three.

In celebration of the Pond-Williams nuptials, I present something old, something new, something borrowed, and something blue.

Start off by borrowing some old ice cube trays from your friends. Drop 3 fresh, newly picked blueberries into each of the ice cube squares. If you want to add a little extra festive color, drop in a pinch of fresh lemon zest. Now fill the tray with water, and freeze. Yes, you're making blueberry ice cubes for your drink. This is a wedding. Be fancy.

Let a few of those trays freeze overnight. The next day, squeeze 1.5 cups/355 milliliters of fresh lemon juice. That's about 8-10 medium sized lemons. For the love of your own tastebuds, do not, under any circumstances, use the vile fraud that is "lemon concentrate." Those plastic squeezy bottles are a crime against humanity.

Put 1 cup/130 grams of berries in a large, microwave safe bowl and mash them gently. Add the sugar and 1 cup/250 milliliters of water. Give everything a good stir, then nuke it for 2 minutes. Stir it again. If the sugar hasn't melted, put it back in the microwave for another minute, then give it another stir. You now have big, sugary bowl of tastiness.

Mash the blueberries a little more. You want to eke out their essence like you're leeching the soul from a gelfling. Let the mix sit for about 10 minutes, stirring occasionally, then strain it into a large pitcher. You want all the tasty goodness with none of the fleshy solids. Throw away the spent, old berries.

Top your pitcher off with the freshly squeezed lemon juice, plus the vodka and the rest of your water. Give it another good stir. You should have a lovely purple colored pitcher of alcoholic goodness. If you'd like it bluer, add a couple drops of food coloring and give it another stir.

To serve, fill one saucer with water and another with your blue sugar. Dip a lowball glass into the water then into the blue sugar in order to rim the glass. Drop in a few of your prepared blueberry ice cubes. Carefully pour in your cocktail. Garnish the glass with a fresh lemon wheel and sprinkle a couple blueberries on top. You can also skewer a few blueberries on a cocktail sword and use that as a second garnish. '

Kazran's Night Sky Fog Cups (S5E14 - A Christmas Carol)

8 cinnamon graham cracker sheets
4 tbsp/57 g butter
2 tbsp/30 g sugar
8 oz/227 g softened cream cheese
1 cup/130 g blueberries
1 cup/100 g whipped cream
juice of 1 lemon
paper fish on toothpicks

It's time for another blatantly steampunk episode of Doctor Who. Luckily, I like 'em like that.

I had such a hard time concentrating on food instead of transcribing all the best one liners, but I climbed halfway out of the dark to bring you this recipe for fish swimming in clouds.

One of the nice things about this Christmas episode is it gives you an excuse to decorate your table with flying fish while lightly sugaring up your guests. If you're wondering why you should decorate your table with flying fish, just trust me. It's this or go to your room and design a new kind of screwdriver. Don't make my mistake.

Put your graham cracker sheets in a plastic bag and beat them like they're a disappointing only son. When your graham crackers are bitter, broken crumbs of their former selves, sweeten them up with the melted butter and sugar until you have a nice dough you can reshape to fit your own ideals.

Divide the graham cracker dough between 8 shot glasses. Really pack it down in there pretty well. Now juice the lemon and beat it into the softened cream cheese. You're welcome to add a couple tablespoons of sugar if you like your desserts a little sweeter. Once your lemony cream cheese is nice and smooth, pack it into the shot glasses like milky white fog topping the dirty brown graham cracker earth below.

Finally, top the shot glasses with whipped cream. If you're a good person, you'll buy whole cream and viciously attack it with a high speed mixer, but we both know you're going to lazily pick up a tub of Cool-Whip and call it a day. Such a disappointment. Sprinkle 4-6 fresh blueberries on top of the Cool-Whip then finish each of your shot glasses with a yellow curl of peel viciously ripped from the flesh of your lemon.

To get the full holiday effect from this episode, print out some brightly colored fish at home (or grab some from a dollar store) Tape them to bamboo skewers cut to different heights and plant the skewers in the middle of your fog cups. Scatter these around the table so it looks like you have flying fish swimming around your party foods.

If you happen to be hosting a Doctor Who theme party in honor of the latest Christmas episode, bring along some Christmas Crackers.

Americans, if you've never played with Christmas crackers, do not let anyone try to convince you they're edible. The "cracker" part comes from the popping sound they make when ripped open. They're not easy to find in the United States, so you now have an excuse to visit Ikea. I promise you won't have to assemble them yourself.

British readers, I hate to break it to you, but unless they're BBC addicts, most Americans thought everything about that Christmas dinner was as authentic as the flying fish.

Both the desert and the Christmas crackers will be equally well received at your Christmases past, present and future.

SERIES SIX: HELLO, SWEETIE

The Doctor's Last Picnic (S6E1 - The Impossible Astronaut)

red wine
red grapes
cheese wedge
strategically wedged sonic screwdriver
picnic basket full of mystery (which, really, you can fill with plenty of other
recipes from this book. For all we know, that basket is bigger on the inside,
so feel free to go nuts.)

Hello, sweetie. Let's be honest. If you want to do this episode justice, a
corner of your table will include a pot of coffee, twelve jammy dodgers, and
a fez, all served on top of a highway roadmap of the United States (see your
local state highway tourist office to get one for free.) It's up to you whether
you serve the jammy dodgers in the fez, but confidentially, you can get cheap
red fezzes at the dollar store.

Honestly, if I knew this was my last meal, I'd have gone a bit fancier. At the
very least, I'd have picked a drink I liked. Maybe The Doctor filled up on
burgers and fries at the Utah diner before taking everyone out to Lake
Silencio. In honor of that, feel free to serve hearty American cheeseburgers
alongside The Doctor's last picnic.

If you're in the mood for something a little less literal than The Doctor's last picnic, try this:

Flaming Canoe Pyre Cocktail

½ shot/22 ml Kahlua
½ shot/22 ml Irish cream
½ shot/22 ml creme de banana
½ shot/22 ml 151 rum
dash cinnamon
banana

Pour your Kahlua, Irish cream, and creme de banana into a large brandy snifter and gently stir them together. Carefully layer the
151 rum on top. Don't stir it. You want this to float above the denser layer. Sprinkle the top with a little cinnamon. (It adds some
drama to the flame.)

Now carefully use a barbecue fire starter or a very long fireplace match to set it on fire. The drink should go up like The Doctor's
pyre, with the cinnamon adding little sparks as it burns. Once the rum burns out, stir everything together with a long slice of banana,
in honor of The Doctor's last party and drink a toast to the last of the Time Lords.

Tardis Blue Fondue with Dippable Spaceships (S6E2 - Day of the Moon)

1 cup/237 ml white wine
2 tbsp/30 g butter
1 tbsp/15 g flour
1 tsp/5 g mustard
7 oz/200 g Gruyere cheese, cubed
7 oz/200 g Cheddar cheese, cubed
7 oz/200 g Emmentaler cheese, cubed
4 shakes Worcestershire sauce
1 tsp/5 ml blue food coloring
1 loaf slightly stale sourdough bread

To really do this episode justice you need to give every guest a sharpie necklace. If they get drunk at your party, have fun putting hash marks on their belly or ankles. When they ask later, profess ignorance. If you're feeling kind (and don't remember the Silents) you could always hand out small black eyeliner pencils on a string instead.

Alternately, as a super-parasite, instead of making any recipes yourself, you could get other people to do it for you then make them forget. Since you're a good host and not one of the Silents, you get to make some Tardisy blue space age fondue for your guests.

You're going to be juggling some pans here. In one small saucepan, bring your wine to a boil. In another one, melt your butter. Sprinkle the flour over the butter and stir constantly. Add in the mustard and Worcestershire sauce. Keep cooking for about five minutes. Now add the food coloring and wine. Stir until everything is free of lumps.

Finally, add in the cheese a little at a time. Keep stirring and adding more cubes until you run out of cheese and have a silky smooth pot. If it's not blue enough, go ahead and add a few more drops, stirring until you have a consistent color. Don't dump all the cheese in at once. Honest. You'll end up with a burned, foul smelling lump on botttom and some rock hard bits on top with an angry cheese magma in between. Take your time melting each handful into the cheesy mass.

Pour the mix into a fondue pot. If you don't have a fondue pot, you can always go the cheap route by pouring it into a crockpot and substituting bamboo barbecue skewers for the fondue forks.

Once you have a home for your blue cheesy melt, cut your loaf of sourdough bread into Apollo 11 triangles with somewhat squared off tops. Serve with sliced green apples, cooked fingerling potatoes, button mushrooms, cherry tomatoes, or your favorite space age fondue dippers. Finish it all off with a tall glass of Tang and a slight sense of paranoia about why you can't find your lost keys.

Curse of the Good Ship *Fancy* Sandwich (S6E3 - The Curse of the Black Spot)

1 large loaf of unsliced Italian bread
1 small bunch romaine lettuce
1/4 cup/60 g mayonnaise
¼ cup/60 g dijon mustard
10 slices your favorite cheese
10 slices roasted red bell peppers
1 lb/455 g sliced deli meat in your choice of flavors
1 bag large pretzel rods
sliced pitted olives
toothpicks

I know you were expecting a rum drink, but this is a whimsical episode and as such, deserves a whimsical recipe. Who could fail to love an edible pirate ship? It feels like something you should eat in a treehouse.

To make your pirate ship, start by cutting twenty evenly spaced slices into your bread. Don't cut all the way through - just go about ¾ of the way down. You don't want your ship to fall apart. Every other cut, line one side of each slice with mayo and the facing side with mustard. You should have a blank slate slice then a condiment filled slice. You want to leave every other slice blank so you can simply cut through it when the time comes to serve your sandwich. That way the part you serve will be nicely seasoned while the part left behind will be nice and dry rather than a sticky mess.

Fill in the condiment smeared slices with a piece of cheese, slice of roasted red bell pepper, and a hunk of your favorite deli lunch meats (I like turkey and roast beef, but use whatever you normally eat.) At this point, you have a rather uninspired group sub sandwich.

Let's make some magic happen.

Peel off three of your nicest looking romaine lettuce leaves. If they're unevenly sized, you want the tallest one in the middle and the ones in front and back to be slightly smaller. Carefully cut two holes in the lettuce leaves and thread the large pretzel rods through them. You now have a sail attached to a mast. Carefully insert your sails into your pirate ship sandwich. For finishing touches, arrange pitted black olive slices as portholes on each slice of the ship. Hold the portholes in place with a toothpick.

You can add a ship steering wheel to the front by cutting a smallish wheel of lemon and pinning it in place with a toothpick.

This looks best served on a large platter surrounded by blue jellybeans with a few gold chocolate coins tossed in for good measure.

Blueberry, Cucumber, and Starfruit Time Scraps (S6E4 - The Doctor's Wife)

1 large cucumber
1 large starfruit
2 cups/260 g blueberries
1 lemon
1 orange
1 lime
2 tbsp/30 ml rice wine vinegar
1 tbsp/15 ml olive oil
1 tsp/5 ml honey
½ tsp/2.5 g salt
pinch cayenne

Hello, sexy. You deserve a dish as blue as the Tardis, full of bright white moons and burning yellow stars with hints of orange and yellow comet trails dashing around your bowl.

If you have fresh blueberries, that's great. If you're relying on frozen, Put them in a colander, put the colander in a bowl, and let them sit in the fridge overnight. Save all the tasty blue juice dripping off of them for use in a cocktail. When you're ready to make the dish, take the berries out first and let them come to room temperature.

Wash any wax off your lemon and orange then carefully zest them both. You want to make sure you only get the brightly colored peels. That interior white pith is nasty and bitter. Toss the zest into a small bowl. Juice the lime into the bowl, next add the rice wine vinegar, olive oil, salt, and cayenne. Whisk them together to make a nice, light citrussy dressing.

Next, peel your cucumber and cut it in half lengthwise. Use a spoon to scoop out the seeds. Angle the edges a bit to make nice, white crescent shapes. Cut the seeded cucumber into moon shaped slices and toss them in a large bowl. Wash the starfruit and cut it into slices the same width as your cucumber moons. Toss them into the same bowl.

The cucumber and starfruit slices are sturdier than the berries, so add the dressing now and toss it about until everything is thoroughly coated. If you're using fresh blueberries, add them now, gently mix them, and call it a day. If you're using frozen berries, rinse them lightly to remove any last bits of leaky juices (this way you won't stain the other fruits) and add them to the fruit bowl.

Top the whole thing off with any leftover zest or some reserved slices of lemon and orange peel, just to add more Tardissy color. This wilts fast, so make it right before your party starts.

If you're in the mood for a fancy dinner party, this is great with some Chicken and Ood soup for Nephew, the Tardis Wellington for Idris, and your choice of blue cocktails.

Confidentially, this is also a good base for a Vincent inspired Starry Night platter.

Melted Rebel Flesh (S6E5 - The Rebel Flesh)

1 lb/455 g russet potatoes
8 cloves garlic
3/4 cup/85 g whole blanched almonds
1/2 cup/120 g extra-virgin olive oil
1/2 cup/120 g water
juice of 1 large lemon
3 tbsp/45 ml white wine vinegar
1 tbsp/15 g kosher salt
½ tsp/2.5 g fresh ground black pepper
1 hardboiled egg
red apple, olive and raisin scraps

I wanted to give you a rebel flesh recipe that would make you cry more, more, more.

Then I remembered that was a Billy Idol lyric and not a Dusty Springfield one. One look at these aliens and I knew exactly what I was going to make. After all, the Flesh looks like sculpted mashed potatoes with hard boiled eggs for eyes. They might as well have included a recipe for Skordalia on the lids of the acid vats.

Peel your potatoes, cube them, and boil them until tender. Drain the potatoes and let them cool slightly. While they're cooling, peel your garlic and toss it in a food processor or blender. Add the almonds, olive oil, salt, and lemon juice. Process it all into a thick paste. Add everything but the potatoes and pulse it a couple more times so everything is nicely mixed. Finally, make sure your potatoes are totally drained then throw them in the blender or food processor along with everything else. Pulse lightly until you have a uniform mass of Flesh colored tasty paste.

Serve your Flesh dip in an oval dish to get the full effect of a melting human face. Cut the hardboiled egg in half and lightly sprinkle it with cayenne pepper to make bloodshot eyes, then position them at the top of the face. Slice your apple, rub it with the remains of your lemon (to stop it from turning brown) and position it for the mouth. If you're good with a knife, try to carve a gaping scream. You can also drop a couple raisins in the middle for barely formed nostrils. This goes well with a tray of vegetables, pita bread wedges, and an existential dread that your memories aren't really your own.

Liquid Flesh Cocktail (S6E6 - The Almost People)

4 pasteurized eggs
2 cups/475 ml Irish whiskey
2 cups/475 ml sweetened, condensed milk
2 cups/475 ml heavy cream
2 tbsp/30 ml chocolate syrup
2 tbsp/30 ml strong, brewed coffee
1 tbsp/15 ml high quality vanilla
1 tbsp/15 ml almond liqueur
1 tbsp/15 ml honey (optional)

The cocktail is my version of homemade Irish Crème Liqueur. If you're feeling lazy, just pick up a bottle of Bailey's and pour it into a decanter. You now have instant Flesh. However, if you've never tried homemade Irish Crème, you are missing out on one of life's great pleasures. This recipe is dirt simple, cheaper than a bottle of Bailey's, and delightfully easy to modify according to tastes. As much as I like the original recipe here, I also really enjoy it with a tablespoon of cinnamon or a quarter cup of peppermint schnapps. Play with it.

Crack the eggs into a blender. Add everything else. Put on the lid and let it enthusiastically blend away until everything is thoroughly integrated. At this point, simply pour it on ice and drink up. That's it. It's almost embarrassingly easy. Your Irish crème will stay good in the fridge for a few days, though mine rarely lasts that long. This is a good time to reuse any of your leftover Last Human Fruit Leather combined with some plain brown bags made into paper dolls for the acid miner jumpsuits. Suddenly, you have a Flesh ganger for everyone at your party and a glass full of liquid flesh for them to drink up.

Headless Monk (S6E7 - A Good Man Goes to War)

Fish:
4 tbsp/60 ml olive oil
4 standard issue lunch-size brown paper bags
4 (6 oz/170 g) halibut, swad, or other white fish fillets
salt and pepper
2 tbsp/30 ml soy sauce
2 tbsp/30 ml freshly squeezed lime juice
3 tbsp/45 g freshly grated ginger

Salsa:
2 ripe mangos, peeled and diced
4 scallions, trimmed and diced
½ red bell pepper, diced
2 tbsp/30 g chopped onion
4 tbsp/60 ml freshly squeezed lime juice
1 tbsp/15 ml rice wine vinegar
1 tsp/5 g salt
½ tsp/2.5 g cayenne pepper.

You could host a party around this episode alone. You get a best-of-aliens parade including everything from the Silurians to the Pirates to the Cybermen However, you get to see something new and awful here in the form of the Headless Monks, so let's celebrate the awkwardness with its own special recipe This makes a great Whovian centerpiece for a sit down dinner. The bags smells delicious while also looking creepily suspicious in the middle of the table .

Start by preheating your oven to 425F/218C. While it heats up, drizzle a tablespoon of olive oil over the outside of your paper bags and rub it in with your hands until the bags are entirely coated. They'll get a little wrinkled. That's okay. Greasing them up helps keep the paper bags from igniting while in the oven. Let the olive oil soak into the paper while you rinse your fish fillets and pat them dry. Generously season both sides of the filets with salt and pepper.

In a small bowl, mix your soy sauce, lime juice, and ginger. Open each bag and put a single fish fillet in the bottom. Carefully reach in and spoon one quarter of the soy-lime mix over each filet. To make the full headless monk effect, bunch the top of the paper bag together and then roll it down, so it looks like the cowl of a robe. Just underneath that, cinch it closed with a rubber band.

Put the bags on a baking sheet and cook the fish for 18-20 minutes. When you take the bags out, tie a rope knot around the neck of each bag to add to the overall headless monk effect. Fluff out the shoulders of the bags before putting them on the table. While your headless monks are baking, mix up your salsa by simply combining all the salsa ingredients in a large bowl and tossing them gently with a fork. To serve, tear a small slit in the bags, carefully transfer the fish to a plate, and top it with the freshly made mango salsa. This pairs very well with the Blueberry, Cucumber and Starfruit Time Scraps.

Regeneration Fizz (S6E8 - Let's Kill Hitler)

1 shot/45 ml banana rum
1 shot/45 ml blue curacao
chilled, pink sweet sparkling wine
lemon twist

Don't get me wrong. I love Moffat's writing, but this episode had plot holes you could drive a starship through. So to help you help you ignore them and just enjoy the amusing one liners and in-references instead, I humbly present this strong regeneration fizz. Drink enough and it will erase your memory.

Simply pour your orange vodka and banana rum into a champagne glass. Top it off with sweet, sparkling wine and garnish the glass with a twist of lemon peel. Menacingly serve it with a banana and a kiss, perhaps while crying a river over the gaping continuity issues. At least it's pretty. This is the perfect drink for a gay gypsy bar mitzvah.

Jammy Dodgers (S6E9 - Night Terrors)

2 cups/450 g unsalted butter, softened
1 cup/220 g firmly packed brown sugar
1 cup/100 g white sugar
2 large eggs
7 1/2 cups/1020 g flour
4 tsp/20 g baking powder
1 tsp/5 g salt
1/4 cup/60 ml milk
1 tbsp/15 ml vanilla extract
1/4 cup/60 g seedless raspberry jam, or seedless
strawberry jam

Have you ever noticed how many episodes feature
giant disembodied eyeballs? It makes me wonder
about what kind of phobias lurk in the minds of the
set designers.

If you're not in a mood to cook, use this episode as an excuse to deck out your table in play food. If, on the other hand, you bought this tome because you were looking for a cookbook instead of the world's third geekiest set of decorating ideas, it's time to sit back with some tea and biscuits (or, for the Americans, milk and cookies).

If there's one thing people are reading for other than fish fingers and custard it has to be jammy dodgers. British readers can stop by the grocery store, but for the Americans, if they want The Doctor's favorite cookie they'll probably have to whip up a batch from scratch.

Start by beating your softened butter with an electric mixer until it's nice and fluffy. Gradually add in the sugars, beating well between each addition. Or, realistically, just dump in all the sugar and keep blending for a long, long time. Once your butter and sugars are a deliciously sweet and fatty mass, add your eggs and just keep beating. Add the vanilla and milk, and once more keep beating until you have a smooth, fatty soup. In another bowl, mix your flour, baking powder, and salt. I bet you can guess what happens next. Gradually add the flour mix to the butter mix, beating enthusiastically all along the way, until the two become a single happy dough.

Divide the dough into four equal parts. Bundle up each ball of dough in plastic wrap and put it in a fridge for at least 3 hours, or overnight.

When your cookie dough is nice and chilly, mash your first lump between two pieces of parchment paper then get a rolling pin or your least favorite canned goods and roll the dough until it's only ⅛ inch/ 0.4 centimeters thick. Cut it into circles using a two inch/5 centimeter round cutter. If you have a small heart shaped cutter, make a little hole in the middle of the cookies. If not, use whatever small circular object you have around your kitchen to cut a small hole in the middle of half the cookies.

Grease up a cookie sheet. Arrange the cookies at least two inches apart and bake them at 350F/180C for 8 - 10 minutes, or until they're a pretty golden brown. Once you take them out of the oven, let the cookies cool completely. Spread the solid cookies with some seedless raspberry jam. Top them with the cutout cookies. Once they're glued together, you can either eat them as they are or dust them with powdered sugar.

Since you're reading a Doctor Who cookbook, you already know to serve the finished cookies in a red fez

Two Streams Garden Cocktail (S6E10 - The Girl Who Waited)

2 shots/90 ml pear vodka
2 tsp/10 ml simple syrup
1 tsp/5 ml fresh squeezed lime juice
1 fresh basil leaf, ripped
1 hibiscus flower
2 dashes orange bitters
soda water
1 firm, fresh pear

In honor of this tearjerker episode, I present an herbal cocktail made from things older Amy found in the Red Waterfall garden at the Two Streams facility.

Put your hibiscus flower at the bottom of a lowball glass. (You can find edible hibiscus flowers at health food stores, upscale groceries, some tea shops, and on Amazon.) Add just enough soda water to completely cover the flower. Meanwhile, add your pear vodka, fresh squeezed lime juice, simple syrup, ripped basil leaf, and orange bitters to a cocktail shaker full of ice. Pound it like you're trying to beat down the walls of time.

Strain the contents of the shaker over your hibiscus flower. Cut a long stick of pear from one side of the fruit and use it as a swizzle stick. Garnish the glass with a curl of green peel cut from the other side of the pear.

Praise His Cheeseball (S6E11 - The God Complex)

10 oz/285 g cream cheese
3 tbsp/45 g sugar
zest of 1 large lemon
4 tsp/20 ml freshly squeezed lemon juice
8 graham crackers

Oh, Rory. You're right. Every time The Doctor gets chummy with someone you really should notify their next of kin. Rita would've made a great companion. After all, she successfully guessed that The Doctor has experience as a professional cheesemaker.

A cheesy 80's hotel would have a cheese and crackers tray sitting outside the restaurant as an enticement to lure diners in. You can whip up a spreadable cheese ball worthy of his praise in less than ten minutes, with no cooking.

Start by mixing the cream cheese and sugar until they're a smooth, uniform paste. Next mix in the lemon juice and lemon zest. Give them an enthusiastic beating until the praising stops. Shape the whole thing into a ball, flatten it slightly on top, and wrap it in plastic wrap. Put it in the fridge for at least three hours, though overnight works just as well.

Before you take it out, put the graham crackers (I like using the cinnamon flavored ones, but you can pick whatever type you like) into a plastic bag and mercilessly beat them with your least favorite canned goods until you have a bag of coarse graham cracker crumbs.

Unwrap your cheese ball. Take a little care re-shaping it if necessary. Now roll it around in the graham crackers until it's well coated. Finish it off by using a mix of cake decorating letters and a couple different colors of icing to write "Praise Him" on top. Refrigerate the whole thing until you're ready to serve it.

Surround the cheese ball with graham crackers, vanilla wafers, and shortbread cookies.

Serve with strong milky tea, because, as Rita says, if you're British, tea how you deal with trauma.

Stormageddon's Cybermat (S6E12- Closing Time)

2 packages refrigerated crescent roll dough
8 tbsp/120 g Nutella
4 tsp/20 g cinnamon
4 tsp/20 g sugar
seedless raspberry jam
edible silver spray paint
1 pair of plastic vampire teeth
aluminum foil
black cake icing

Craig is back! And The Doctor is "here to help." Stormageddon, dark lord of all, wants to put everything he sees in his mouth, including Bitey the Cybermat. In order to keep the Cybermat from eating his face, I've concocted a perfectly safe version that will taste great with all that milk the boys kept buying throughout the episode.

Mix your cinnamon and sugar together in a small bowl. Now put your Nutella in the microwave and nuke it for 15-20 seconds to soften it up for easy spreading.

You'll make your Cybermat in two main parts - the body and the head.

For the body, simply spread a tablespoon of Nutella inside a crescent roll. Sprinkle it with a teaspoon of the cinnamon-sugar mix. Roll the back of the body into a long, tapered, Cybermat tail. To make the head, once more spread a triangle of dough with Nutella and sprinkle it with a teaspoon of cinnamon sugar. Mash up a piece of aluminum foil about the same size as your plastic teeth. Carefully wrap the second crescent around the teeth, leaving the mouth open, in order to form the big, rounded head. Tuck the tail in the back of the head and pinch the dough together.

You should end up with 8 Cybermats. Grease up a cookie sheet and bake the crescents according to their package directions. When they come out, coat the Cybermats with your edible silver spray paint. Work fast, because you want to remove the aluminum foil plug and replace it with the plastic vampire teeth while the dough is still warm and malleable.

Once the teeth are in place, touch up the edible silver spray paint, then let the Cybermats cool. When they're room temperature, put a few tablespoons of seedless red raspberry jelly in a microwave for a few seconds to soften it. Use a paintbrush, pastry brush, or your very careful fingers to paint on three red stripes along each side of the tail to symbolize the glowing red interior we could see when the Cybermat moved. Use icing to paint a big, black eye on either side of the head, taking care to give it the characteristic Cyberman eye teardrop.

These are best served ominously peering at the world from inside a dollar store cowboy hat.

Texting and Scones (S6E13 - The Wedding of River Song)

Orange Blueberry Scones:
2 cups/260 g fresh blueberries
2 cups/276 g flour, plus more for rolling berries
1 tbsp/15 g baking powder
1 tsp/5 g salt
1/3 cup/67 g sugar
1/4 cup/58 g unsalted butter
3/4 cup/178 ml heavy cream
1 egg

Orange Glaze:
2 tbsp/30 g unsalted butter
2 cups/180 g powdered sugar, sifted
2 oranges, juiced and zested

I keep trying to write a recipe with the Silents, but every time I look away from my computer I forget all the ingredients. Instead, I consent and gladly give you this recipe for orange blueberry scones. they're full of Tardissy colors to keep your taste buds interested while you nervously text your date.

Preheat oven to 400F/205C.

In one bowl, mix your flour, baking powder, salt, and sugar until they're well blended. Cut your butter into cubes and crumble it into the dry mix until you have something that looks like buttery crumbs.

If you're a good person, you'll whisk your heavy cream and egg together in another bowl before dumping them into the flour mixture Realistically, we know you're not going to do that. Try to mix everything in pretty well, but don't go crazy with it. If you overwork the dough, you'll end up with a tough, rubbery, uncooperative final product.

In yet another bowl, roll your blueberries around in flour. The flour should hopefully keep your berries from all sinking straight to the bottom of the scone while baking. If you're using fresh blueberries, they might not stick as well. If you're using frozen, make sure to drain them thoroughly in a colander before adding them to the flour. The flour will stick better, but the berries will be a lot more fragile.

Once your berries are floured, gently fold them into the scone dough. Try not to bruise them too much.

Get a baking sheet nice and greasy. Go ahead and grease up your hands with a little extra butter. Now scoop out a couple tablespoons of dough and shape it into a rough triangle before putting it on the sheet. Try to arrange your scones at least a couple inches apart. Bake the scones for 15 to 20 minutes, or until they turn a nice golden brown. You'll want to shove one right in your mouth, but they're best off if you let them cool before dousing them in tasty orange glaze.

The orange glaze is pretty quick and easy to make. Some people use a double boiler, but honestly, I just throw the butter, sugar, and orange juice into a microwave safe bowl. Cook for 30 seconds, stir heartily, cook another 30 seconds, and stir again. Keep it up until the butter and sugar are melted together and the mix has thickened up into a syruppy goodness. When your glaze is ready, stir in the orange zest.

Generously douse the scones with glaze. Now once more, leave them alone. Walk away while they harden. In an hour, they'll be as firm as your resolve. If you've been looking for just the right way to ask a Whovian out on a date, hand them one of these and ask if they're interested in texting and scones. If they don't get the reference, keep looking. If they do, you're about to have a very good night.

Wartime Christmas Fruit Cake (S6E14 - The Doctor, The Widow and the Wardrobe)

1 ¼ cups/170 g flour
3 tsp/15 g of baking powder
1 tsp/5 g baking soda
1/2 tsp/2.5 g allspice
½ tsp/2.5 g cinnamon
pinch salt
1 cup/240 ml very strong tea
6 tbsp/90 g margarine or butter
6 tbsp/90 g sugar
6 tbsp/90 g dried fruit

This is the sort of Christmas cake a good British mom like Madge would've made her family during the war. Due to rationing, it was made without eggs. You can add one now to act as an extra bit of food glue, or you can make it as-is and surprise your vegan friends with a dessert they can actually eat.

As an added bonus, if you bake it in a couple of large, round cans instead of in a loaf pan you even get some nice, alien tree shaped heads which are easy enough to sculpt into the face of a tree king and queen when you're finished.

Put a kettle on. You're going to want half a pint (1 cup, for Americans) of good, strong, black tea. Have a cup of tea for yourself and pour another one in a sauce pan. Add the sugar, margarine (butter was rare and expensive during the war) and dried fruit of your choice to the pot. Simmer it all together for about 3 minutes, or until the sugar is completely melted.

Meanwhile, mix the flour, salt, baking powder and baking soda in a large bowl. Give the tea mix a couple of minutes to cool down, then pour it over your flour mix. Beat it thoroughly. You want to not only make sure everything is well mixed, but also hopefully get a little air into the dough.

Grease the inside of two large, clean aluminum cans. It doesn't matter what was in them before, as long as one end is still intact and the paper has been completely removed. If your largest cans are only 15 oz/440 gram sized, you may need to split the batter into four portions instead of two. Regardless of size, grease them up well, spoon the batter in until your cans are ⅔ full, then put them in the middle of a 350F/180C oven for 45 minutes (for the large cans) or 30-35 minutes for the smaller ones. Check for doneness by sticking a long toothpick or thin bamboo skewer down into the middle. If it comes out clean, your cakes are done. If not, bake them for another 3-4 minutes and test them again.

Let the cakes cool for at least 20 minutes after you remove them from the oven. If you greased the cans well enough, they should slide out. If you didn't, you can always take a can opener to the bottoms and use the newly cut lid to gently push the cakes all the way through.

The fruit cakes should be moister than you expect. Use your fingers to sort of pinch the surface into a vague face shape. Remember, it's easier to push in than pull out. Once you're satisfied with your tree face, use the tines of a fork to cut bark lines all around the exterior of each face. Leave them out to dry overnight and the surface will dehydrate a bit and get slightly more crusty. (Although honestly, they taste better when they're completely moist).

Once your guests have admired the Christmas tree aliens, simply cut the cakes into nice round slices about an inch wide. It's a more merciful end than melting them in acid rain.

These are best served with a pat of butter or margarine, strong, hot tea for the adults, and lemonade on tap for the kids.

FISH FINGERS AND CUSTARD

Let's be honest. If you're in the UK, all you really need to do is pick up a box each of fish fingers and custard. Pop the fish fingers in the oven, pour a bowl of custard, and you're good to go.

This is a little more complicated for Americans. For some reason, our chicken have fingers but our fish comes in sticks. The protein isn't a problem, but we don't sell pourable custard. Most people substitute vanilla pudding instead. For those of you in the UK, what we call pudding is like an eggless custard made so thick it's practically a solid.

Everyone wants the look of fish fingers and custard on their Whovian table, but not all fans are equally enamored with the taste. This chapter offersome passable alternatives so you can achieve the right look with a less whimsical taste.

British Style Custard

1 cup/250ml milk
½ cup/125ml double cream
1 tbsp/15 g sugar
2 tsp/10 g cornstarch
1/2 teaspoon/2.5 ml vanilla extract
3 extra large egg yolks

Most Americans have never had the kind of pourable custard The Doctor drinks. The closest thing we have is vanilla pudding. To Americans, "pudding" is kind of like a less eggy, more sweet custard made so thick it'll hold a spoon upright. The Doctor's dessert was just as mysterious to us as real Root Beer is to you. Sure, you've heard of it. You've even seen it on television. But taste and texture are still a mystery.

Psst...Americans. Join me over here in the corner for a second. Listen, if your friends have never had the custard sauce folks in the United Kingdom take for granted, you can make a quick and dirty substitute by adding an extra cup and a half of milk to a box of instant vanilla pudding mix. Yes, I said a cup and a half. This is supposed to be a pourable sauce. I swear I'm not making this up. Instead of icing, people in the UK pour this on top of cakes. Honest.

Ahem. The rest of you can rejoin us, now. Everyone who can simply walk into a grocery store and buy a box of pre-made custard probably has a family recipe passed down from your grandmother. You should either get your custard from a box or make hers. The rest of you can give this recipe a try. Like most things made from actual ingredients instead of a chemical cocktail, it won't be as flamboyantly yellow as The Doctor's custard. Add a few drops of yellow and orange food coloring to get the full televised cheap box of processed custard look.

To make your custard, start by mixing the sugar and cornstarch in a bowl. Pour in the milk and whisk it all together. Meanwhile, pour your cream into a saucepan and gently warm it over a medium heat. Don't boil it. As the cream warms, gradually whisk in the milk mix.

Once you've poured in all your milk, keep whisking. If you stop whisking, your custard will develop lumps and a skin and other disturbingly organic things that make you think it's about to rise out of the pot like animated Flesh.

When your heavily whisked mix comes to a boil, pull it off the heat. In another bowl, beat your eggs until they're smooth. Gradually add the egg mix to the milk, whisking heavily as you add it in. Don't just dump all your eggs in at once. You'll end up with an overly sweetened and mostly inedible egg drop soup.

Once your eggs and milk are all playing nicely together, put the pan back on a medium heat. Add the vanilla. All that whisking you've done? Keep it up. You want to ever so slowly bring your mix back up to a boil. Once it starts to bubble, yank it off the heat and keep stirring for another minute. You can serve it hot or pour it into a bowl, wrap the bowl in plastic wrap to prevent it from growing a disturbing skin and potential sentience, and enjoy it anytime you'd like for 2-3 days

Quick and Easy Pound Cake Faux Fish Fingers

1 store bought pound cake
2 cups store bought graham cracker crumbs
2 egg whites
½ cup/125 ml heavy cream
1 tsp/5 g cinnamon
½ tsp/2.5 ml vanilla
butter

Preheat your oven to 400F/205C. Start by carefully cutting your store bought pound cake into fish finger shaped rectangles about 1 inch/2.5 centimeters thick by 4 inches/10 centimeters long. Aggressively butter the bottom of a baking sheet in preparation.

Pour your egg whites, heavy cream, cinnamon and vanilla into a bowl and whip them up. Set up a nice assembly line with your pound cake, cream mix, and graham cracker crumbs.

Quickly dunk each slice of pound cake into the cream mix. Immediately roll it in the graham crackers. Place each strip on the buttered baking sheet. See, they're looking more like fish fingers already.

Bake the whole mess for 7-8 minutes. Flip the faux fish fingers then bake them for another 5-7 minutes. You'll end up with a crunchy rectangle that looks just like boxed fish fingers but tastes like sweet, crunchy cake.

Gooey Brownie Faux Fish Fingers

boxed brownie mix
vanilla wafers
gingersnaps

These are a good alternative for people who prefer their sweet, faux fish fingers on the chocolaty side.

Prepare the brownie mix according to the package instructions. However, under bake them by 3-5 minutes. You want your brownies to be solid enough to stay together, but delightfully gooey in the center.

While the brownies are baking, mix 4 cups/500 grams of vanilla wafers with 1 cup/125 grams of gingersnaps. The different colors and textures add to the natural look of the fish fingers. Toss the cookies into a blender or food processor and grind them into breadcrumb sized pieces.

Once the brownies have cooled, cut them into fish finger shaped rectangles. The nice thing about the moist, gooey interior is it should hold onto the cookie crumbs without needing some extra form of food glue (like an egg white wash). Roll the brownie rectangles in the cookie crumbs, making sure to get all sides. Your best results will probably come from middle pieces since they have more moist interior surface area. If your crumbs aren't sticking to the edge pieces, go ahead and trim the crust then try again.

Serve these with the sweet custard substitute of your choice.

French Toast Fish Fingers with Whipped Maple Syrup Custard

French Toast:
1 loaf of stale bread cut into thick rectangles
3 eggs
½ cup/125 ml milk
2 tsp/10 ml vanilla
1 tsp/5 g cinnamon
½ tsp/2.5 g salt

Maple Cream "Custard"
1 cup/250 ml heavy whipping cream
¼ cup/75 ml maple syrup
8 drops yellow food coloring
3-4 drops orange food coloring

Americans can simply buy a box of frozen French Toast strips, a box of frozen vanilla flavored Cool Whip, some maple syrup, and some yellow food coloring. Bake the French Toast, mix the rest of it, and voila - breakfast sweets with a Whovian twist.

If you live outside the United States, what we call French Toast is probably an alien concept. It's made from stale bread refreshed by a good dunking in eggs and milk then topped with a sweet maple-inspired syrup. The advantage here is that grilled bread just so happens to look an awful lot like every other fried, breaded food.

To make these French Toast sticks look the most like fish fingers, use an unsliced loaf of dense bread. Cut the bread into fish finger sized rectangles. You can let the slices sit out overnight if you want to get a crunchier exterior.

Mix the eggs, milk, vanilla, cinnamon and salt in a bowl. Beat it enthusiastically until everything is well blended.

Meanwhile, because decadent breakfast sweets are meant to be delicious, melt a tablespoon/15 grams of butter in a skillet over medium heat. Dip your bread rectangles in the egg mix. Let them soak for a couple seconds (longer if the bread is properly stale) and arrange them in the skillet. You want to turn them every 3-4 minutes, making sure to cook all four sides until golden brown. Feel free to add more butter when you turn them.

Once you've cooked all of your faux fish sticks, it's time to make your tasty custard substitute. Considering I've already extolled the virtues of butter, it should come as no surprise we're topping this with real, delicious, fatty cream. Honestly, real fish fingers and custard would probably be healthier, but who cares as long as it's delicious?

Pour your whipping cream, maple syrup, and food coloring into a large bowl. If the shade of yellow isn't custardy enough for you, add a couple more drops of food coloring. Once you're satisfied, beat the contents with a hand mixer until they magically transform from a liquid to a fluffy solid.

This fish fingers and custard substitute is equally good for breakfast or dessert.

Toasted Cornbread Fish Sticks with Honey Butter Custard Dip

Cornbread:
1 cup/140 g flour
1 cup/140 g cornmeal
1 tsp/5 g baking soda
1 1/2 tsp/7.5 g baking powder
1/2 tsp/2.5 g salt
2 eggs, well beaten
1 cup/125 ml buttermilk (or ¾ cup/95 ml Greek yogurt and ¼ cup/30 ml whole milk)
2 cups/500 ml whole milk
1 ½ / 23 g tablespoons butter

Honey Butter "Custard"
1 cup/225 g butter
½ cup/170 g honey

The first half of this recipe is pretty darn easy. Start by preheating your oven to 400F/205C and greasing up a 9x9 inch/23x23(ish) centimeter square baking pan.

Mix all your dry ingredients in a great big bowl. Once they're all playing nicely together, add in your wet ingredients. If you live outside the United States, you may have difficulty finding buttermilk. Don't panic. Just substitute the yogurt and milk mix instead. You'll be fine. Stir it all up until it goes from being lumpy to merely being grainy. Once the batter is as smooth as it's likely to get, pour it into your greased pan. See, I told you cornbread was easy. Bake it for 20 to 25 minutes, or until the top is golden brown and a toothpick inserted in the middle comes out clean.

Now comes the hard part. Once you take it out of the oven, you have to wait for it to cool. If you don't, it'll turn into a crumbly mess that won't hold a shape. If you want some unexpectedly tasty fake fish fingers, now is the time to practice your patience.

Let's pretend you didn't turn into screaming rage monster after cutting away one corner and discovering it crumbled into gold dust in your hand. No, in this alternate reality, you walked away for a few hours, maybe watched the last couple Christmas specials, and when you came back your beautiful loaf of cornbread was cool and waiting.

To avenge the anger of your alternate universe self, the time has come to take a knife to your loaf. Use a sharp blade to cut it into fish finger sized rectangles. Now stop and admire them. Honestly, if you were lazy, you could just pile those on a plate and call it a day. Luckily, unlike your alternate universe double, you're ambitious.

Toss a couple tablespoons of butter into a medium-hot skillet. Now carefully fry up each side of the cornbread until it's a nice, toasty golden brown. It's amazing how much the toasting transforms your cornbread from yellow food sticks to passable breaded fish fingers.

While those are frying, put your room temperature butter in a large bowl. Add the honey and attack it with a hand mixer. You want to get a lot of air into the butter so it'll have a nice whipped texture, which makes it a lot more custard-like. If you want it even more liquidy, go ahead and add a quarter cup of plain yogurt. You can add a couple drops of yellow and orange food coloring as well to give it that final custardy kick.

Feel free to supercharge your honey butter's flavor by adding a teaspoon of orange zest OR a teaspoon of lemon zest OR a teaspoon each of cinnamon and vanilla. If you go for the cinnamon and vanilla, you'll need more food coloring to compensate.

These do have a tendency to fall apart faster than the other fake fish fingers, so don't use them as an impromptu baton when conducting an imaginary orchestra.

Fish Custard Tacos

prepared fish fingers of your choice
tortillas
coleslaw
honey-mustard dressing (optional)

Mango Salsa:
2 chopped, peeled mangoes
1/2 cucumber, seeded and chopped
2 tbsp/30 g red onion, diced
1/3 cup/100 ml pineapple juice
2 tbsp/30 g honey
juice of 1 lime
½ tsp/2.5 g cayenne pepper (optional)
½ tsp/2.5 g salt
2 tbsp/30 g corn starch

This incredibly forgiving recipe lets you enjoy the look of fish fingers and custard while providing an actual edible entree.

Fish tacos are incredibly popular in Texas, California, and the American border states in between. The rest of the world finds the whole concept a bit iffy - until that first bite.

To make these, mix your pineapple juice, lime juice, honey, pepper, and salt in a bowl. Carefully sprinkle in your corn starch. Spread the corn starch out as much as you can to avoid lumps. Once the corn starch is sprinkled over the liquids, whisk it in until everything is completely blended and free from lumps. Now all you have to do is add in your diced mangoes, cucumbers, and onions. Give it all a good stir so the solids are all coated in your sauce then set it all aside to thicken slightly.

While the salsa thickens, make the fish fingers of your choice. You can use any of the gazillion recipes online or you can just buy a box of breaded fishy goodness at the grocery store. I'm not here to judge. Just make sure you have some kind of warm and crunchy sea based protein on the table.

When you're ready to eat, simply spread a little honey mustard dressing on the tortilla (some fish taco lovers will call you a heathen while others say you're doing it just right), add your fish fingers, and spoon some mango salsa and coleslaw. You can make the coleslaw from scratch using the Baked Hath recipe or just buy some from the grocery store. You're now holding your first fish taco.

I love serving fish tacos at Whovian gatherings. You get all the fun of actual fish fingers and real custard on the table, but when it comes time to eat, you can dip cookie or cake into the custard while assembling your fish fingers into a nice main course fish taco. Everybody wins.

Savory Fish Fingers and Custard Mock Cake

prepared fish fingers
toasted Panko breadcrumbs
1 8 oz/225 g package cream cheese
1/2 cup/125 g mayonnaise
4 tbsp/60 g Dijon mustard
4 tsp/20 g curry powder
1 tsp/5 g turmeric
1 tsp/5 g honey
1 tsp/5 g salt

You can go two ways with this. The obvious one is to decorate some cake like a stack of fish fingers and ice it with a thick, dark yellow custard substitute.

Let's do it the hard way instead.

To make this as cake-like as possible, you need to make the "icing" nice and thick. What you're really making here is a honey mustard dipping sauce with a curry kick. The cream cheese is both a bulk filler and a fluffing agent.

Put your cream cheese, mayonnaise, mustard, curry powder, honey, and salt into a blender or food processor and whip it into a frenzy of faux filling goodness. However long you think is enough, just keep going. You want to get as much air in there as possible in order to build up bulk and keep it from being too drippy. If your fake custard isn't yellow enough, add another 1/2 teaspoon of turmeric and keep whipping it.

While your "custard" is whipping, bake your choice of fish sticks. It's entirely up to you whether these come from a box or are homemade, but considering what you're about to do with them, I suggest you go cheap and buy a box from the grocery store.

Once your fish fingers are nice and crunchy, spritz a cookie sheet with nonstick spray and spread a thin layer of panko bread crumbs across it. Toast these at 400F/205C for 3-4 minutes to get them extra crunchy.

Now all you have to do is assemble your cake. Make a nice cake sized square of fish fingers. Top it with a layer of your honey mustard filling. Add another layer of fish fingers, preferably oriented in the opposite direction, followed by another layer of fake custard. Keep this up until you run out of fish fingers. Save enough of the filling to lightly coat the top and sides. Once you have a gold brown square of protein, carefully take your toasted panko bread crumbs and use them to coat the top and sides so it looks like you made a tasty cake with a graham cracker crust.

As you can probably guess, this gets soggy fast. You want to serve it as quickly as possible. If it sits on the table all night long, you're going to have bemusingly atmospheric fish mush. While it's still warm, cut it into nice, cake-like squares and serve to your surprised guests. If they're in on the joke, just let people pull fish sticks off the pile at their leisure.

Fish Fingers and Custard Cocktail

1 shot/45 ml cupcake flavored vodka
1 shot/45 ml vanilla vodka
1 shot/45 ml heavy cream
2 drops yellow food coloring
1 drop orange food coloring
graham cracker crumbs

If you don't have any spare graham cracker crumbs hiding in a cupboard, throw a couple graham crackers into a plastic sandwich bag and smash them into crumbs using your bottle of cupcake vodka. Once you have a nice crumbly mess, empty it into a saucer. Tip a bit of heavy cream into an adjacent saucer. In this age of fat free recipes, you probably only bought the cream for this drink. You can afford to waste a little.

Dip the rim of your martini glass in the saucer of milk then grind it into the saucer full of graham cracker crumbs. See, rimming really is more fun than you expected.

You can't leave a lovely glass like that empty. Pour your cupcake vodka, vanilla vodka, heavy cream into a cocktail shaker full of ice. If you really want that full artificial custard color, add in a couple drops of yellow and one drop of orange food coloring. Shake like your Tardis is tumbling through a time vortex. When you have your feet back under you, carefully strain the contents into your nicely rimmed martini glass.

Garnish it with the sweet faux fish finger of your choice and offer it to the nearest archaeologist with a reminder that your heart, among other things, is bigger on the inside.

Savory Mock Custards

A lot of people make sweet fake fish fingers which they can dip into the tasty goodness of actual custard. Sometimes, though, you don't want to sugar your guests up like two year olds at Halloween. if you're in the mood for something savory, these five easy sauces should give you the glossy yellow look of custard with a savory flavor that goes well with your fish fingers. They're not all silky smooth, but the fake fish fingers from the sweet dishes aren't necessarily fooling anyone, either.

The best thing about these recipes is that they're fast. You can whip up any of them in less time than it takes to empty a box of frozen fish fingers on a tray and pop them in the oven. They make for a quick, cheap, instantly recognizable Whovian meal. What more could a busy host want?

Curry Mayonnaise Mock Custard

1 cup/450 grams mayonnaise
4 tbsp/60 g plain Greek yogurt
4 tbsp/60 g mango chutney
2 tsp/10 g yellow curry powder
1 tsp/5 g turmeric
1 tsp/5 g honey
¼ tsp/healthy pinch ginger powder
juice of 1 lime

Mix the turmeric, curry powder, and mayonnaise until you have a consistent color. If it's not yellow enough to pass for custard, add one drop of orange and two drops of yellow food coloring, then give it another good stir. Once you're happy with the color, mix in everything else. For a smoother, more custardy texture, put everything into a blender or food processor. This is equally good on chicken strips or as a sandwich spread.

Tartar Sauce Mock Custard

1 cup/450 g mayonnaise
2 tbsp/30 g sweet pickle relish
2 tsp/10 g prepared yellow mustard
2 tsp/10 g fresh squeezed lemon juice
1 tsp/5 g turmeric powder

Mix the turmeric and mayonnaise until they're well blended. The end result should be about the color of custard. If not, add a pinch more turmeric and give it another good hearty stir. Now simply mix in everything else until you have a nice, uniform custardy consistency. The pickle relish will make this a little lumpy. You can put it in a blender to smooth it out, but I prefer to suffer through a less than perfect look for the sake of the pleasant texture from the pickles.

Lemon Dill Herbed Mock Custard

1 cup/450 g mayonnaise
1 tbsp/15 g dried dill
2 tsp/10 g garlic powder
2 tsp/10 g onion powder
2 lemons, zested and juiced
2 drops yellow food coloring
1 drops orange food coloring

You're probably spotting a pattern by now. Once more, mix the mayonnaise and food coloring. If you're satisfied with the custard-ness of the color, dump in everything else. If not, experiment with the food coloring and more mayo until you're happy with the color. After that, simply mix everything else into the colored mayo and give it all a good stir. It'll be a little chunkier than your average custard, but the dill flavor is worth it.

Horseradish and Mustard Mock Custard

1 cup/450 g mayonnaise
2 tbsp/30 g dijon mustard
2 tsp/10 g prepared white horseradish
1 tsp/5 g turmeric
juice of ½ lemon
pinch salt

The turmeric and mustard give this a nicely custardy color without having to resort to dyes. To make a batch, simply dump everything in a bowl and mix it enthusiastically until you have a smooth paste. Serve it with the fish fingers of your choice.

Honey Mustard Mock Custard

1 cup/450 g mayonnaise
¼ cup/85 g honey
¼ cup/70 g dijon mustard
1 tbsp/15 g yellow mustard
2 tbsp/30 ml rice wine vinegar
1 tsp/5 g turmeric
½ tsp/2.5 g salt

Once more, simply dump everything into a bowl. Enthusiastically mix it together until your sauce reaches a uniform custard-like color and texture. If you prefer it sweeter, feel free to add more honey. This doesn't taste or look anything like the honey mustard dipping sauce you get from fast food restaurants, which are mostly made from corn syrup and chemical factory runoff. Instead, despite the color, this tastes suspiciously like real food. You've been warned.

APPENDIX

MAIN COURSES

51 - Baked Hath Served Over Black Beans and Topped With a Red and Green Cabbage Slaw (Series 4, Episode 7)
25 - Coronation Chicken (Series 2, Episode 8)
63 - Cool Bow Tie Pasta with Protesting Star Whale Brains (Series 2, Episode 2)
79 - Curse of the Good Ship Fancy Sandwich (Series 6, Episode 3)
91 - Fish Custard Tacos (Series 6, Episode 1)
33 - Fishy Daleks (Series 2, Episode 14)
82 - Headless Monk (Series 6, Episode 7)
29 - L.I.N.D.A.'s Tardis Wellington (Series 2, Episode 11)
64 - Open Faced Dalek Ironsides (Series 5, Episode 3)
55 - River Song (Series 4, Episode 10)
92 - Savory Fish Fingers and Custard Mock Cake (Series 6, Episode 1)
11 - Slitheen Killing Beans on Toast (Series 1, Episode 4)
36 - Shakespearian Shooter Sandwich (Series 3, Episode 3)
60 - Squash Stingrays (Series 4, Episode 16)
54 - Vashta Nerada Detection Kit (Series 4, Episode 9)
67 - Vampire Space Fish (Series 6, Episode 6)
15 - Wartime Cheese and Potato Dumplings with Fried Spam Slices (Series 1, Episodes 9-10)
43 - Weeping Angel Wings (Series 3, Episode 11)

APPETIZERS AND SIDE DISHES

28 - Black Hole Mezze (Series 2, Episode 10)\
80 - Blueberry, Cucumber and Starfruit Time Scraps (Series 6, Episode 4)
25 - Chicken and Ood Soup (Series 2, Episode 9)
32 - Cyberman Ghosts (Series 2, Episode 13)
58 - Dalek Caan's Corn (Series 4, Episode 14)
21 - Deffry Vale School Chips with Krillitane Oil (Series 2, Episode 4)
77 - The Doctor's Last Picnic (Series 6, Episode 1)
56 - Donna's Time Beetle (Series 4, Episode 12)
38 - Extermination Loaf (Series 3, Episode 5)
48 - Marble Circuits with Fire Dipping Sauce (Series 4, Episode 13)
61 - The Master's Drums (Series 4, Episode 18)
81 - Melted Rebel Flesh (Series 6, Episode 5)
62 - The New Doctor's Rubbish Plate (Series 5, Episode 1)
49 - Ood Mezze Plate (Series 4, Episode 4)
44 - Professor Yana's Gluten Neutrino Map Binder (Series 3, Episode 12)
74 - Rory the Roman's Faro Stew (Series 5, Episode 12)
13 - Satellite 5 Mystery Takeout Noodles (Series 1, Episode 7)
69 - Silurian Hot House Salad with Lemon-Lime Vinaigrette (Series 5, Episode 8)
16 - Slitheen Eggs (Series 1, Episode 11)
50 - Sontaran Soldiers (Series 4, Episode 5)
53 - Timelord Cyanide Detox Platter (Series 4, Episode 8)
71 - Vincent's Rustic Potatoes (Series 5, Episode 10)

SNACKS

12 - Banana Dalek (Series 1, Episode 6)
44 - Cucumber Drums of Madness (Series 3, Episode 13)
56 - Dalek Invasion Ships (Series 4, Episode 13)
19 - The Doctor's Hand (Series 2, Episode 1)
72 - The Doctor's Omelet (Series 5, Episode 11)
37 - Kitty Nurse Kibble (Series 3, Episode 4)
9 - The Last Human Fruit Leather (Series 2, Episode 2)
11 - Slitheen Skin Suits (Series 1, Episode 5)

ADULT BEVERAGES

75 - Blueberry Lemonade Wedding Punch (Series 5, Episode 13)
10 - Charles Dickens Own Christmas Punch (Series 1, Episode 3)
51 - Clone Vat Cocktail (Series 4, Episode 6)
23 - Cybus Brain Cleansing Cocktail (Series 2, Episode 6)
22 - The Doctor's Accidental Banana Daiquiri (Series 2, Episode 5)
42 - Family of Blood(y Mary) (Series 3, Episode 10)
93 - Fish Fingers and Custard Cocktail (Series 6, Episode 1)
61 - The Fizzy Waters of Mars Cocktail (Series 4, Episode 17)
34 - Huon Particle Cocktail (Series 3, Episode 1)
58 - Jackson Lake Cocktail (Series 4, Episode 15)
81 - Liquid Flesh Cocktail (Series 6, Episode 6)
8 - Nestene Consciousness (Series 1, Episode 1)
20 - New Earth Apple Grass Cocktail (Series 2, Episode 2)
14 - Pete Tyler's Health Tonic (Series 1, Episode 8)
82 - Regeneration Fizz (Series 6, Episode 8)
56 - Sapphire Cliff Cockatil (Series 4, Episode 11)
46 - Titanic 1st Class Menu Punch Romaine (Series 4, Episode 1)
85 - Two Streams Garden Cocktail (Series 6, Episode 10)
20 - Queen Victoria's Nightcap (Series 2, Episode 3)

DESSERTS

21 - 2012 Olympic Shortbread Medallions (Series 2, Episode 12)
66 - Angel Wing Cookies (Series 5, Episode 5)
17 - Big Brother House Bad Wolf Brand Human Chow Cookies (Series 1, Episode 12)
87 - British Style Custard (Series 6, Episode 1)
40 - Burnt Custard (Series 3, Episode 8)
69 - Cinnamon Pull Apart Crack in the Wall (Series 5, Episode 9)
89 - French Toast Fish Fingers with Whipped Maple Syrup Custard (Series 6, Episode 1)
88 - Gooey Brownie Faux Fish Fingers (Series 6, Episode 1)
65 - Irradiated Angels (Series 5, Episode 4)
84 - Jammy Dodgers (Series 6, Episode 9)
76 - Kazran's Night Sky Fog Cups (Series 5, Episode 14)
35 - Moon Cake Pops (Series 2, Episode 2)
88 - Quick and Easy Faux Fish Fingers (Series 6, Episode 1)
41 - Scarecrow Soldiers (Series 3, Episode 9)
86 - Stormageddon's Cybermat (Series 6, Episode 12)
87 - Texting and Scones (Series 6, Episode 13)
88 - Wartime Christmas Fruit Cake (Series 6, Episode 14)
24 - White Chocolate Cybermen Heads (Series 2, Episode 7)

OTHER

46 - Adipose Herbed Butter (Series 4, Episode 2)
45 - Cantaloupe Toclafane (Series 3, Episode 14)
39 - Dalek Sek's Head (Series 3, Episode 7)
68 - Ledweth's Eknodine Pensioners (Series 5, Episode 7)
48 - Marble Circuits with Fire Dipping Sauce (Series 4, Episode 13)
18 - The Mad Dalek Emperor's All Seeing Eye (Series 1, Episode 13)
85 - Praise His Cheeseball (Series 6, Episode 11)
94 - Savory Mock Custards (Series 6, Episode 1)
78 - Tardis Blue Fondue with Dippable Spaceships (Series 6, Episode 2)
90 - Toasted Cornbread Fish Sticks with Honey Butter Custard Dip (Series 6, Episode 1)

VEGAN

12 - Banana Dalek (Series 1, Episode 6)
28 - Black Hole Mezze (Series 2, Episode 10)
45 - Cantaloupe Toclafane (Series 3, Episode 14)
58 - Dalek Caan's Corn (Series 4, Episode 14)
21 - Deffry Vale School Chips with Krillitane Oil (Series 2, Episode 4)
56 - Donna's Time Beetle (Series 4, Episode 12)
9 - The Last Human Fruit Leather (Series 2, Episode 2)
68 - Ledweth's Eknodine Pensioners (Series 5, Episode 7)
48 - Marble Circuits with Fire Dipping Sauce (Series 4, Episode 13)
44 - Professor Yana's Gluten Neutrino Map Binder (Series 3, Episode 12)
13 - Satellite 5 Mystery Takeout Noodles (Series 1, Episode 7)
69 - Silurian Hot House Salad with Lemon-Lime Vinaigrette (Series 5, Episode 8)
50 - Sontaran Soldiers (Series 4, Episode 5)

VEGETARIAN

63 - Cool Bow Tie Pasta with Protesting Star Whale Brains (Series 2, Episode 2)
44 - Cucumber Drums of Madness (Series 3, Episode 13)
32 - Cyberman Ghosts (Series 2, Episode 13)
38 - Extermination Loaf (Series 3, Episode 5)
37 - Kitty Nurse Kibble (Series 3, Episode 4)
9 - The Last Human Fruit Leather (Series 2, Episode 2)
61 - The Master's Drums (Series 4, Episode 18)
81 - Melted Rebel Flesh (Series 6, Episode 5
64 - Open Faced Dalek Ironsides (Series 5, Episode 3)
55 - River Song (Series 4, Episode 10)
16 - Slitheen Eggs (Series 1, Episode 11)
11 - Slitheen Killing Beans on Toast (Series 1, Episode 4)
11 - Slitheen Skin Suits (Series 1, Episode 5)
60 - Squash Stingrays (Series 4, Episode 16)
71 - Vincent's Rustic Potatoes (Series 5, Episode 10)

CELIAC/WHEAT ALLERGY

12 - Banana Dalek (Series 1, Episode 6)
28 - Black Hole Mezze (Series 2, Episode 10)
45 - Cantaloupe Toclafane (Series 3, Episode 14)
44 - Cucumber Drums of Madness (Series 3, Episode 13)

58 - Dalek Caan's Corn (Series 4, Episode 14)
21 - Deffry Vale School Chips with Krillitane Oil (Series 2, Episode 4)
72 - The Doctor's Omelet (Series 5, Episode 11) (without lunchmeat)
56 - Donna's Time Beetle (Series 4, Episode 12)
82 - Headless Monk (Series 6, Episode 7)
9 - The Last Human Fruit Leather (Series 2, Episode 2)
68 - Ledweth's Eknodine Pensioners (Series 5, Episode 7)
81 - Melted Rebel Flesh (Series 6, Episode 5)
74 - Rory the Roman's Faro Stew (Series 5, Episode 12)
69 - Silurian Hot House Salad with Lemon-Lime Vinaigrette (Series 5, Episode 8)
16 - Slitheen Eggs (Series 1, Episode 11) (without pasta)
11 - Slitheen Skin Suits (Series 1, Episode 5)
50 - Sontaran Soldiers (Series 4, Episode 5)
60 - Squash Stingrays (Series 4, Episode 16)
71 - Vincent's Rustic Potatoes (Series 5, Episode 10)

PALEO/LOW CARB

28 - Black Hole Mezze (Series 2, Episode 10)
72 - The Doctor's Omelet (Series 5, Episode 11)
56 - Donna's Time Beetle (Series 4, Episode 12)
9 - The Last Human Fruit Leather (Series 2, Episode 2)
68 - Ledweth's Eknodine Pensioners (Series 5, Episode 7)
69 - Silurian Hot House Salad with Lemon-Lime Vinaigrette (Series 5, Episode 8)
11 - Slitheen Skin Suits (Series 1, Episode 5)
60 - Squash Stingrays (Series 4, Episode 16)